OTTAWA BOOK EXPO
AND OTTAWA FAIR CATALOGUE OF
VENDORS OCTOBER 2019

Edited by
Peter Tremblay

Agora Books

Agora Books

Ottawa, Canada

Ottawa Book Expo and Ottawa Fair Catalogue of Vendors 2019

c. 2019 by Peter Tremblay

Agora Books

P.O. Box 24191

300 Eagleson Road

Kanata, Ontario K2M 2C3   CANADA

Agora Books is a self-publishing agency for authors that was launched by The Agora Cosmopolitan which is a registered not-for-profit corporation.

ISBN: 978-1-927538-47-0

Printed in Canada

Contents

* Booth numbers have been modified for the purposes of this Ottawa Book Expo catalogue.

code | Promoting every child's right to read

EVENT SPONSOR

For the last 60 years, CODE has been working towards our vision of a literate world. The groundwork was laid in 1959, when a small group of educators, librarians and publishing professionals launched the "Books for the developing world" project, packaging unused books in tea chests for shipping overseas. Since then, CODE has grown into Canada's leading international development agency focused uniquely on education and literacy.

Our mission

CODE's mission is to enable student learning by increasing their access to qualified educators and locally-relevant, high quality learning materials.

Our vision

CODE envisions a world where every young person can pursue their education and realize their full potential as a literate, empowered, self-reliant citizen.

Our core values

CODE's work is guided by five core values: human rights, accountability, transparency, fairness, and sustainability.

Partage Vanier

Partage Vanier is the local food bank located at 161 Marier Avenue. The mission statement is to gather and distribute quality food, other necessities of life and resources to individuals and families in need of Vanier.

Mayor Jim Watson at Ottawa Book Expo

957 elmnt fm
The Spirit of Ottawa

OFFICIAL SPONSOR

Pronounced "element," the station is helmed by Aboriginal Peoples Television Network (APTN) and will soft-launch later this summer in Toronto on 106.5FM (and in Ottawa on 95.7FM in mid-July).

The CRTC granted ELMNT its Toronto and Ottawa licenses last June, and APTN has been actively working on the station since then.

"Not only has [Canadian radio] dropped the ball [on Indigenous music], but you have to wonder what is it about, for example, Murray Porter, who is an amazing blues artist, that the blues stations don't play him?" says Jean La Rose, Chief Executive Officer of APTN speaking over the phone from the Banff World Media Festival. "That's where we think ELMNT will make such a huge difference."

La Rose says ELMNT.FM has forged a "really strong partnership with Corus radio," which will provide ELMNT space in its Toronto and Ottawa studios.

Indigenous talent will be driving ELMNT in front of, and behind, the mic.

Thanjai Restaurant

Hailing from the states of Tamil Nadu, Kerala, Karnataka and Andhra Pradesh, Thanjai's dishes offer Ottawa the opportunity to sample the healthy, vibrant flavours of South India. Favouring the use of different spices over excessive oil, South Indian cuisine satisfies taste buds while minding waistlines!

City Councilor Mathieu Fleury and Author Jen Pretty.

Renaissance Press

https://pressesrenaissancepress.ca

Renaissance was founded in May 2013 by a group of friends who wanted to publish and market those stories which don't always fit neatly in a genre, or a niche, or a demographic. We weren't sure what we wanted to publish exactly, so like the happy panbibliophiles that we are, we opened our submissions, with no other personal guideline than finding a Canadian book we would fall in love with enough that we would want to publish and sell.

Five years later, this is still very true; however, we've also noticed an interesting trend in what we tended to publish. It turns out that we are naturally drawn to the voices of those who are members of a marginalized group (people with disabilities, LGBTQIAPP2+ people, people of colour), and these are the voices we want to continue to uplift.

At Renaissance, we treat our authors like family. We are all authors and artists ourselves, and know that their books are their babies. With Renaissance, the authors are involved in every step of the process and their input is highly valued, though devoted committees take on the difficult tasks of copy editing, designing and marketing to achieve professional results. The authors are asked to do a minimal part of the marketing (for example, sharing our social media posts, inviting their circles to the launch, participating in blog

tours) and will receive guidance and help every step of the way.

At Renaissance, we do things differently. We are passionate about books, and we care as much about our authors enjoying the publishing process as we do about our readers enjoying a great, professional quality and affordable product on the platform they prefer.

Nothing Without Us
We are the heroes, not the sidekicks.

"Can you recommend fiction that has main characters who are like us?" This is a question we who are disabled, Deaf, neurodiverse, Spoonie, and/or who manage mental illness ask way too often. Typically, we're faced with stories about us crafted by people who really don't get us. We're turned into pathetic, tragic souls; we merely exist to inspire the abled main characters to thrive; or even worse, we're to overcome "what's wrong with us" and be cured.

Nothing Without Us combines both realistic and speculative fiction, starring protagonists who are written "by us and for us." From hospital halls to jungle villages, from within the fantastical plane to deep into outer space, our heroes take us on a journey, make us think, and prompt us to cheer them on.

These are bold tales, told in our voices, which are important for everyone to experience.

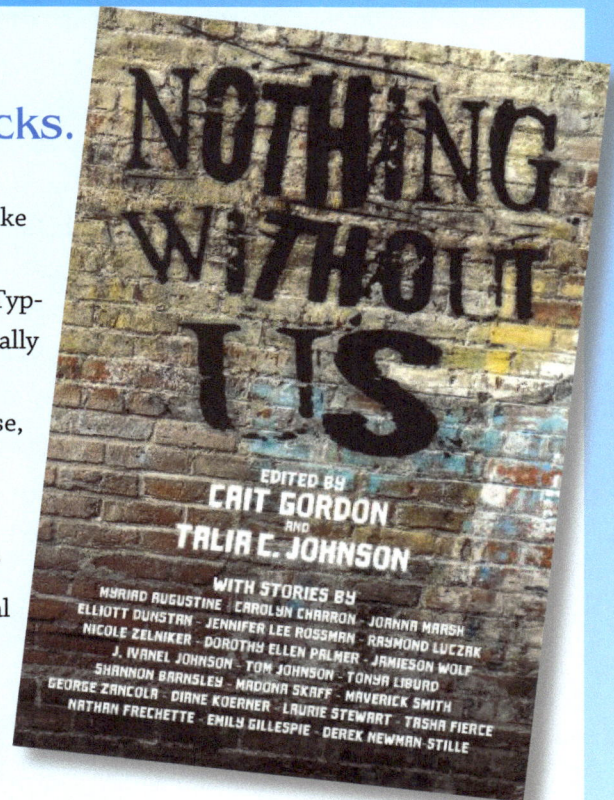

Drummer Eric with Mayor Jim Watson

Skylark

by S. M. Carrière

Earth, 2404 AD Much of Canada has been annexed by an alien force known as the daemon.

Raised in a Vancouver ghetto on the edge of daemon territory, Bennejin Skye is adopted into the United Space Corps and becomes the commander of the highly successful, if somewhat maverick, Strategic Team 6. When the outermost interstellar Way Station suddenly ceases communications with Earth, Commander Skye and Team 6 are sent to investigate. They discover a new alien threat—the insectoid Ragnar, who move through space consuming resources like a virus. Humanity and daemon-kind realize they must unite in the fight to protect Earth. However, there are those within the United Council who believe this aggressor is daemon, and this faction will go to any length to rid Earth of her newest inhabitants.

Overpowered within the United Council, Commander Skye and Strategic Team 6 must turn rogue to save the alliance, or Earth and all who call it home are doomed.

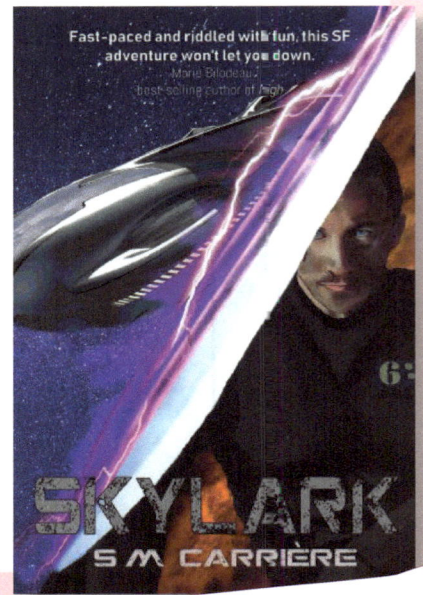

"A military space adventure where Canadian soldiers face their Daemons, Skylark is truly S.M Carrière at her best. I could read it over and over."

Cait Gordon,
author of Life in the 'Cosm and The Stealth Lovers

"Fast-paced and riddled with fun, this SF adventure won't let you down."

Marie Bilodeau,
best-selling author of Nigh

The Wayward Spider

by John Hass

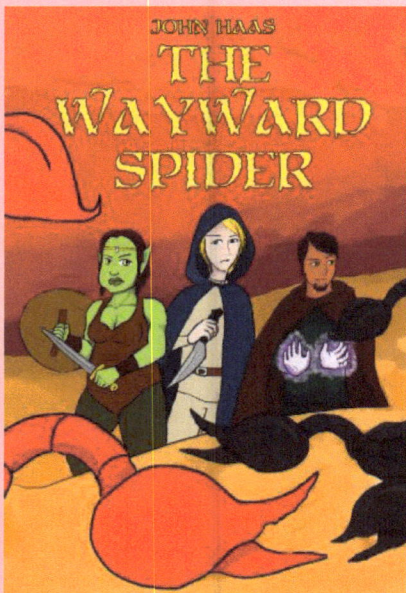

All Spider wants is to seek his fortune as a thief. Is that too much to ask? Must be, since a break in gone wrong leaves him babysitting a powerful magic-user with sporadic control over his spells, and even less of a grip on functioning in society. And that's just where it starts. Each misadventure takes Spider further from his goals, but he's about to learn that sometimes we get what we need instead of what we want.

Werewolves, cults, ghosts and gods. This one has it all. Join a moody thief, a caster of chaos magic and a hulking behemoth as circumstances throw them from one quest to another.

And just why is that ancient cult chasing them?

Run J Run

by Su J Sokol

Jeremy, a high school English teacher coming to grips with a shattered marriage and haunted by the brother he lost, unexpectedly falls in love with his best friend, Zak.

Attractive, wildly unconventional, and happy in an open relationship with his partner Annie, Zak seems to embody everything missing from Jeremy's life, but when the arrest and death of a marginalized student at the Brooklyn high school where they both teach trigger Zak's mental breakdown and slow descent, Jeremy and Annie are compelled to cross boundaries, both external and internal, in a desperate attempt to save him.

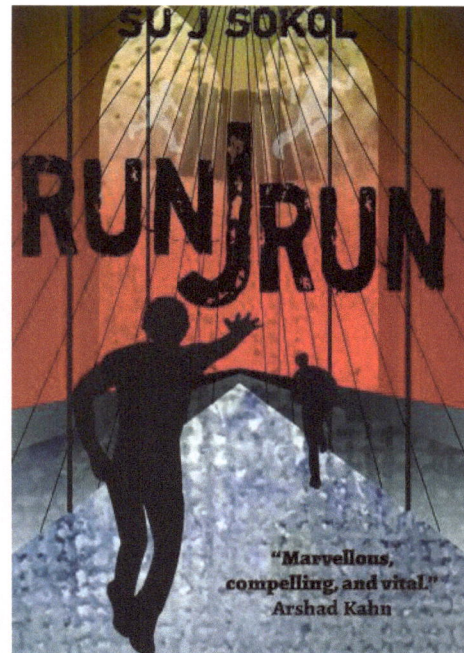

"This gripping story, written with a great deal of graphic detail, compassion, drama, and a detailed sense of place, takes us into the deepest recesses of trauma and makes us look at family and therapy in unconventional but convincing ways. It is intricately plotted and unpredictable."

H. Nigel Thomas, author of No Safeguards, finalist for the Paragraphe Hugh MacLennan Prize for fiction

"Run J Run is a compelling chronicle of a tumultuous, erotically charged friendship imperilled by madness. Sokol charts these struggles expertly and compassionately, even as her narrative pushes buttons, defies categories and conventions, and breaks rules...."

David Demchuk, author of The Bone Mother, nominee for the Giller Prize and winner of the Sunburst Award for Excellence in Canadian Fiction of the Fantastic

"Sokol dares to go to that unexplored place where mental illness intersects with the complexities of sexuality and the result is surprisingly hopeful. The book's social critique is not lost in abstract theory but is solidly rooted in character. There are living breathing people here."

Barry Webster, author of The Lava in My Bones, finalist for the Lambda Literary Award

"Run J Run is a sophisticated depiction of sexual awakening and mental illness. It seamlessly navigates the deeply personal and political with a scopious understanding of the human psyche. Marvellous, compelling and vital."

Arshad Kahn, filmmaker

Laurie Campbell Press

Fiona Flying Fox
Special Agent and the Mystery at the Rainbow Zoo

StoryTellerLaurie.com

Why are the feathers and fur of the birds and animals at the Rainbow Zoo turning pink and purple? Has the food been tampered with, or is it a virus? The fear of the unknown is at the heart of this story. Fiona's investigation reveals that sometimes the source of a problem, is closer to home, than one expects to find.

Soft Cover Edition, 2015
ISBN 978-1-77084-612-8
Printed and Bound in Victoria, BC, Canada
30 pages, Ages 8-10

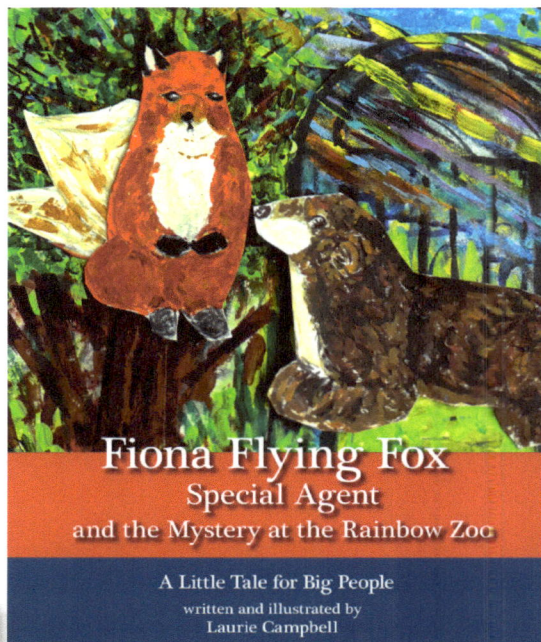

Flying Pigs, Horse Flies and the Big Rain
A Little Tale for Big People

It is summer and there is a heat wave on the farm. How hot is it for the animals? It's so hot that Buster the brown Tabby Cat wants to jump out of his fur.

There has been no rain since the spring. Noah the Goat prays for rain.

A storm comes and life becomes topsy-turvy for the farm animals. On the day of the big rain, Pigs will fly!

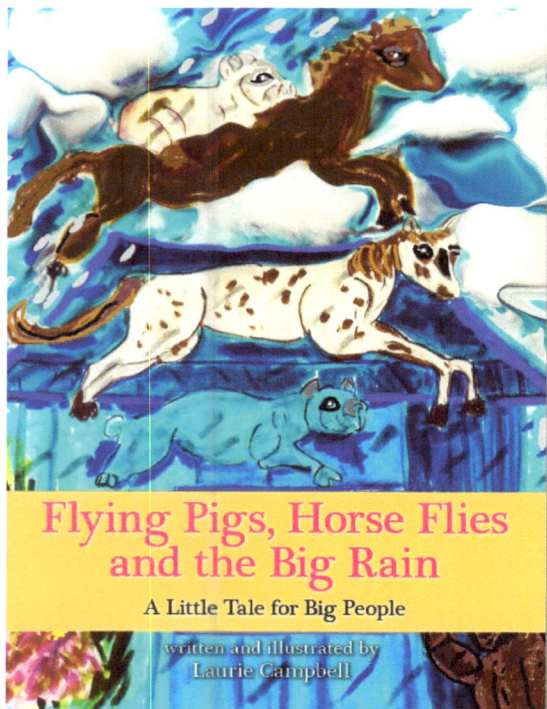

What Do Teddy Bears Eat?

Making healthy food, can be simple and fun for the young. Sharing with your friends and their bears, makes it even better!

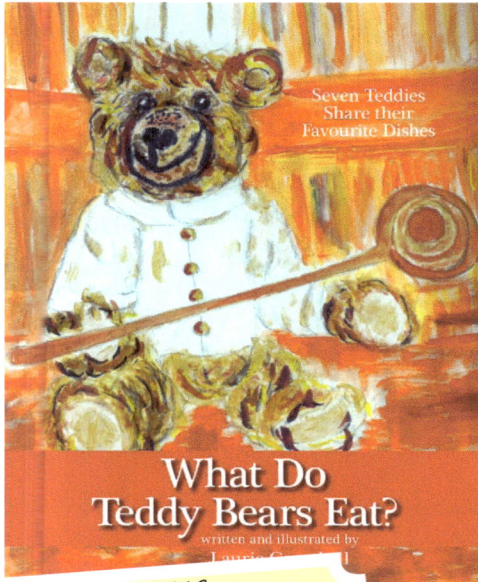

Soft Cover Edition, 2016
ISBN 978-1-77084-750-7
Printed and Bound in Victoria, BC, Canada
28 pages Ages 5-8

Follow the Wind
Gordon and the Northern Lights

This is the story of Gordon, a Moose who lives in British Columbia.
Gordon likes to travel and follows the Wind to find the Northern Lights. But the Wind can blow in all four directions.
It's enough to make a Moose dizzy. Gordon loses his footing, and falls into the Columbia River which takes him south to Oregon.
Gordon travels by boat, sailing ship, and train to reach the Northern Lights.
He encounters human marvels, and makes new friends at the Red Onion Juice Bar in Skagway. One is Karen a Moose, and together they share an out of the world experience.

Soft Cover Edition, 2018
ISBN 978-0-2285-0138-1
Printed and Bound in Victoria, BC, Canada
by First Choice Books & Victoria Bindery
40 pages, Ages 7-10

Laurie Campbell

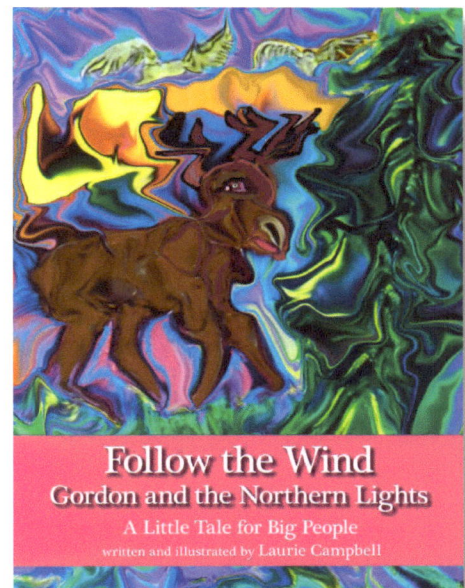

Vivienne Sollows

Author and musician

Mayor Jim Watson

City Councilor
Mathieu Fleury

Susan Jennings

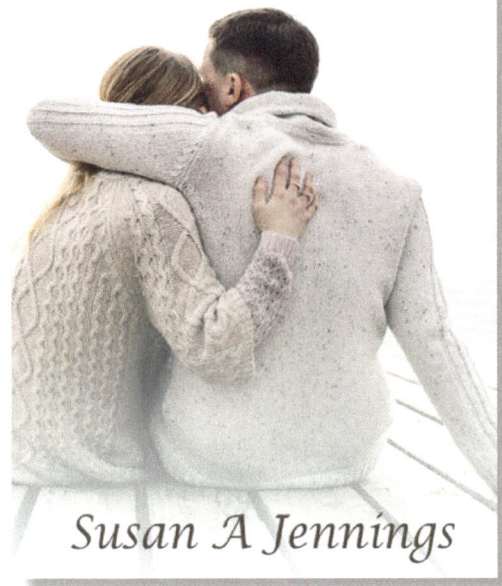

Susan A. Jennings was born in Britain of a Canadian mother and British father. Both her Canadian and British heritages are often featured in her stories. She lives in Ottawa, Canada where she writes, historical fiction always with a love story and contemporary romance. Susan is also the current president of the Ottawa Independent Writers (OIW).

The Narrowboat Romance Series
- Contemporary romance. Book 1

When Love Ends Romance Begins - Shattered by divorce, Katie a once happy stay-at-home mom is lost. All she has left to love is Buddy-Boy, her fluffy, white dog. She never imagined she could find love again or own a successful B&B in an idyllic British village. Book 2 Christmas at Lavender Cottage - A delightful story of romance, a deceitful guests, and a wonderful warm family Christmas dinner and a happy ending.

When *Love Ends Romance Begins*
Book 1 - The Narrowboat Romance Series

Susan A Jennings

The Sackville Hotel Trilogy

Historical saga of love, courage and heartbreak, spanning three decades, two continents and three generations. Book 1 The Blue Pendant, Book 2 Anna's Legacy, Book 3 Sarah's Choice. A determined young Anna defies British Edwardian society, resists marriage, but loves passionately twice. The trilogy is filled with romance, modern history, and Anna's story stretches from the Edwardian era to the Cold war of the 60s.

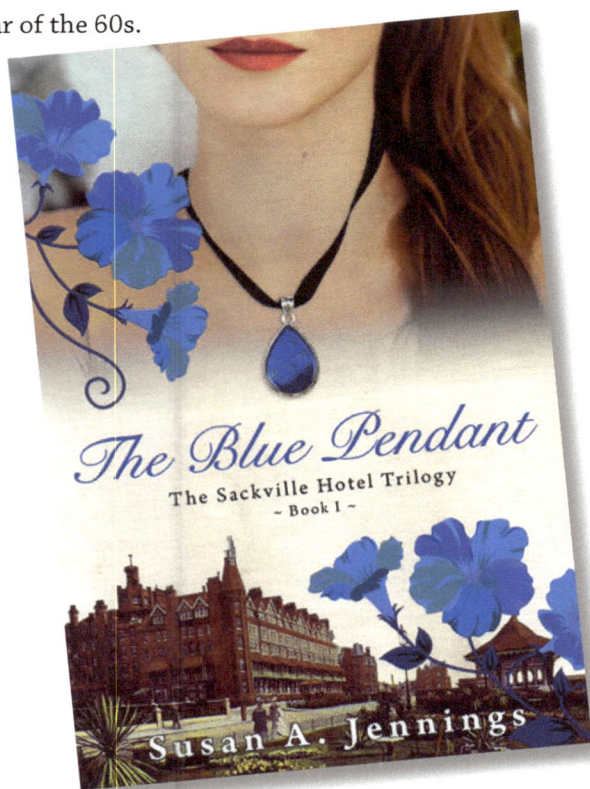

Sophie Series - Historical WW1 - Book 1
Prelude to Sophie's War

A captivating WW1 historical novel of love and loss. 1915, London cowers under bomb attacks from German Zeppelins. Innocent Londoners join shell-shocked, battle-weary soldiers at Bartley Hospital. Nurse Sophie Romano battles her own demons as she comforts others, risking her nursing career and losing the man she loves.

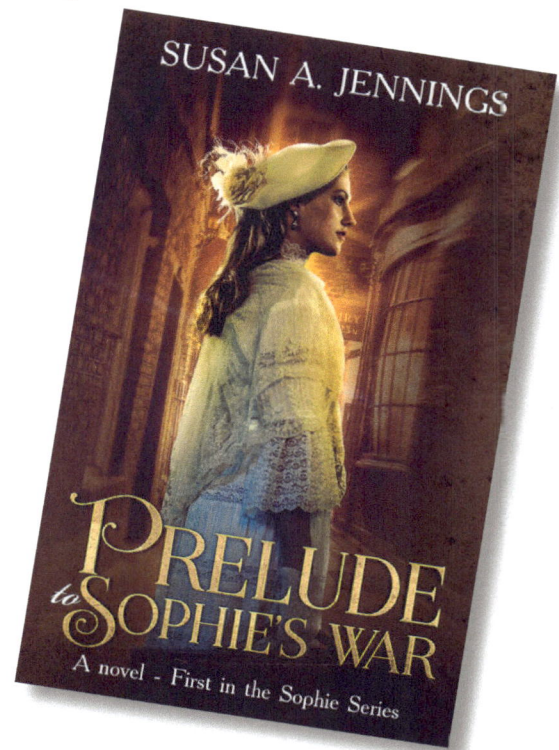

Save Some For Me

A tornado lasting twenty years went through my life. A memoir of an abused and abandoned young wife, the serious hardships of single motherhood of five children and the funny adventures dating as a single mom of five.

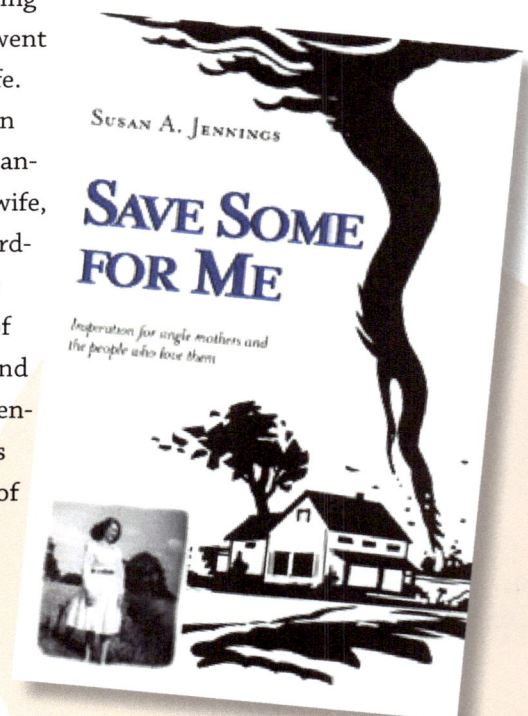

Roger Landriault

Jesus, Son of God or rabble-rouser
Paperback – April 26, 2019

by Roger Landriault

The result of over a decade of research using analytic and comparative reading techniques of the New Testament, searches in ancient documents and apocryphal manuscripts as well as an analysis of the etymology of the names of the characters who have come into contact with Jesus, not only allowed for their true identities to be revealed but also served to establish that Jesus was a married man and father, who with his brothers and sisters had given themselves the political mission to expel the Romans from Palestine.

Unable to convince their fellow Galileans, the dozen revolutionaries decided to confront the Roman authorities in Jerusalem where they were thrown into prison for participating in a riot during which an assassination was committed. As the main instigator, Jesus went through a criminal trial in which he was charged, found guilty and sentenced to death on the cross.

And that's where his story should have ended... What happened after his death? Archaeological discoveries, an analysis of the order in which the New Testament texts were written and research into first century AD traditions have revealed evidence that help shed light on what happened the day following his death and after.

This new reading highlights the inconsistencies of the legends of the Church who preferred to ignore the man that was Jesus in favor of the deified Christ of the Gospels. With Jesus, Son of God or rabble-rouser... the author delivers a methodical, rigorous and controversial study that will not fail to challenge.

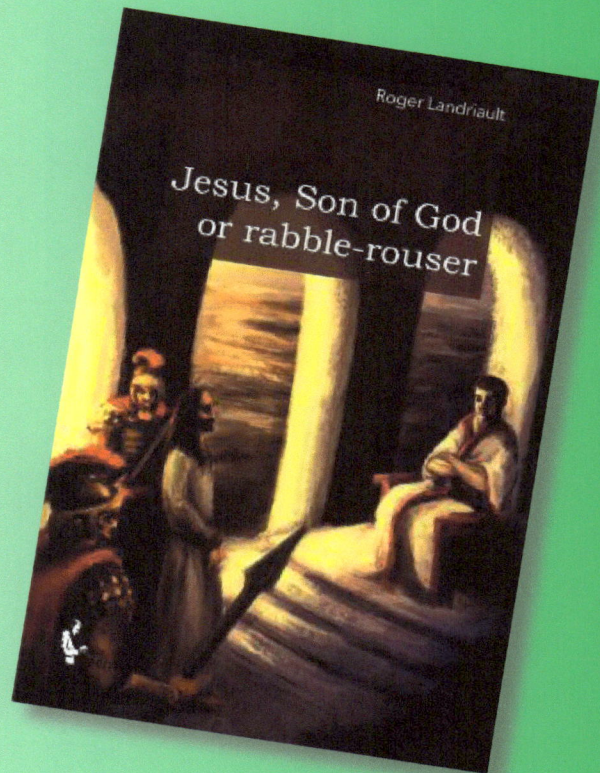

Sylvie Rancourt

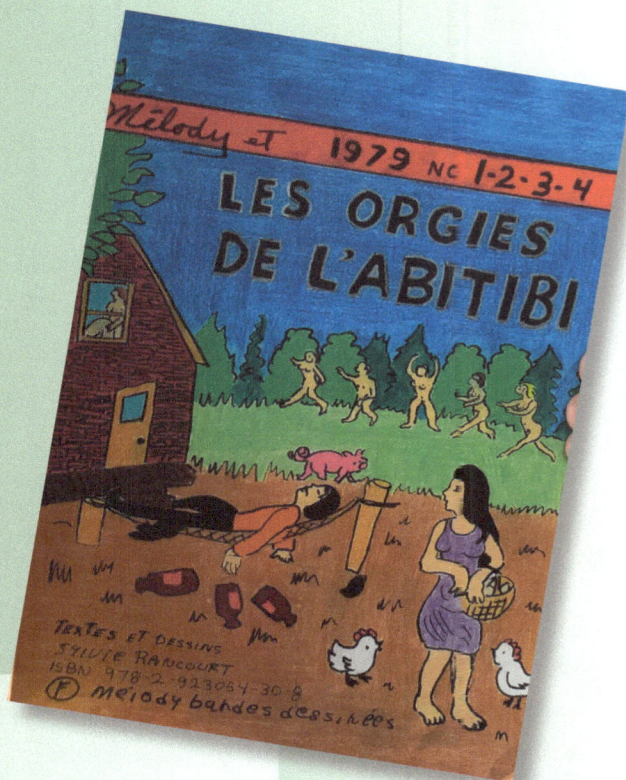

Le premier livre (les orgie de labitibi): je suis nee en abitibi et a 20 ans avec des copain ont a fait des orgies pour passer le temp et se desennuyer.

Le deuzieme livre (lintegral) : Puis .. je suis partie a Montreal et jai commencer a danser nue dans les bars et jai ecrit ma vie sur ce metier de danseuse nue .

Si Señor Restaurant

From the streets of Mexico to Ottawa, our food will connect your memories to your last trip or introduce you to new flavours. Homemade salsas, traditional dishes and "real tacos" made with fresh ingredients.

Anne Raina

Anne Raina is the youngest of ten children. Her father and seven of her siblings spent years in the Royal Ottawa Sanatorium for the treatment of tuberculosis (TB) in the 1930s, '40s and '50s. Her father and her eldest and youngest brothers died of the disease. Her sister, Clara, entered the Sanatorium in 1939 when she was twelve years old and she was discharged in 1952 when she had turned twenty-six.

Anne has been writing since she was a child. While previously published in magazines and newspapers, her first book was *Clara's Rib: A True Story of a Young Girl Growing up in a Tuberculosis Hospital* (anneraina.ca) To date, 4,200 copies of that book have been sold, mainly in the Ottawa area. Brief speaking tours to Canada's eastern and western provinces and to Saranac Lake, USA, drew large enthusiastic audiences.

In November 2015 she published two children's books, *The Kangaroo With The Wooden Shoe* and *Things That Go SPLAT!* The overwhelming response to these books led to her publishing sequels to each in November, 2016 – *The Kangaroo With The Wooden Shoe – Book Two* and *Things That Go Where They Shouldn't*. She is currently working on her mother's biography for publication.

Anne is in high demand as a speaker at schools and libraries and a wide variety of community groups and societies. She has been invited as a keynote speaker at medical conferences and presented annually for a number of years to the first year medical students at Ottawa University Medical School.

Anne was a senior executive with a national disability organization when struck with multiple disabling autoimmune disorders herself. She resides in Ottawa with her husband, Grant Cameron. Her daughter lives in Ottawa, her son in Perth and her stepson in California.

www.anneraina.ca
anneraina@rogers.com

The Kangaroo With The Wooden Shoe

The Kangaroo With The Wooden Shoe is a delightful rhyming tale that readily activates children's imaginations. Young readers enthusiastically become part of the adventure. Teachers and parents are drawn to this interactive book.

The imaginative illustrations, by Julia Taylor, invite young readers along with Kelly Anne and Mark and their curious Kangaroo on multiple adventures. As they accompany them on a camping trip, to school, and attending a concert, children eagerly imagine scenarios of where they might take The *Kangaroo With The Wooden Shoe*.

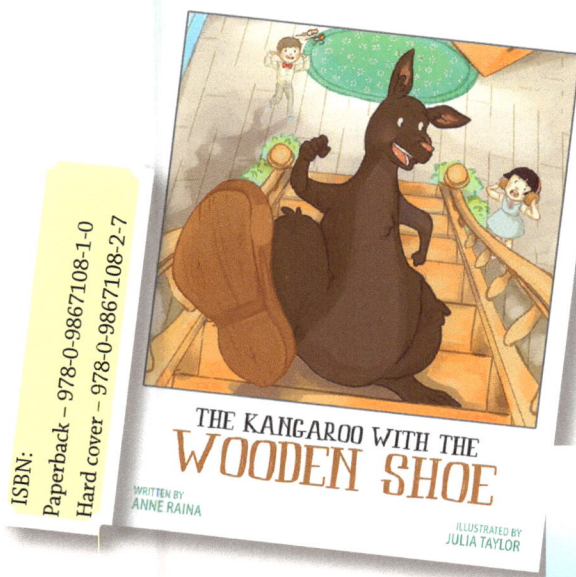

ISBN:
Paperback – 978-0-9867108-1-0
Hard cover – 978-0-9867108-2-7

Clara's Rib:
A True Story of a Young Girl Growing up in a Tuberculosis Hospital

Clara's Rib is the true story of a young girl coming of age in a tuberculosis hospital in the 1940s and '50s. Clara's story focuses mainly on her years growing up in 'the San' in Ottawa, Canada. Readers of all ages will be drawn into the evolving seasons of Clara's life of courage, faith, pranks, laughter, first love, despair and hope from the time she enters the San as a pre-teen until her departure as a young woman in her mid-twenties. Clara, the fourth eldest of ten children, was forced to exchange the daily camaraderie of her big, close-knit family for an even larger family in a hospital filled with TB patients. Discover why, when Clara left the San for the last time, one of her own ribs was packed in her suitcase.

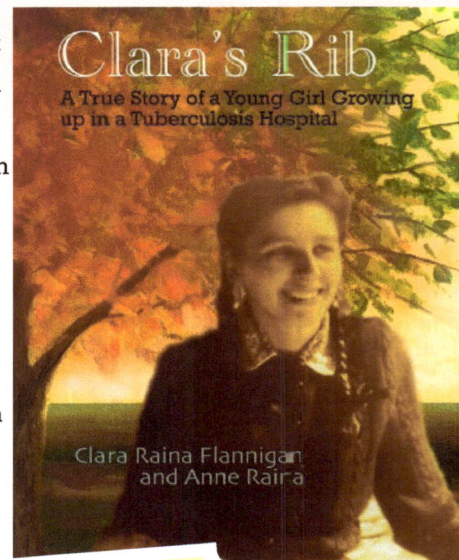

ISBN 978-0-9867-108-0-3

Things That Go SPLAT!

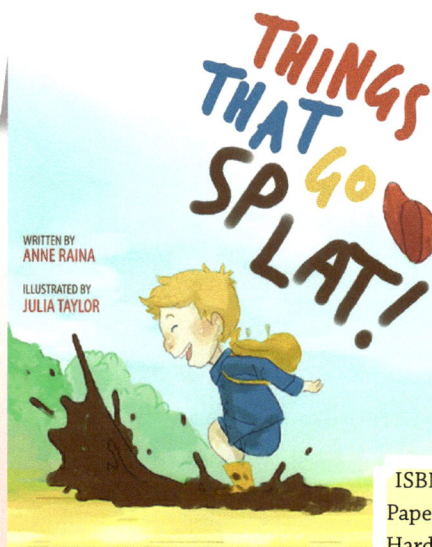

Young readers joyfully embrace this humorous rhyming tale that relates the quest of a mischievous boy to find *Things That Go SPLAT!* The SPLAT! of his toothpaste before leaving for school sets Jacob's imagination

ISBN:
Paperback – 978-0-9867108-3-4
Hardcover – 978-0-9867108-4-1

racing. Dropping an egg on the floor and jumping in a mud puddle lead to more SPLAT! adventures.

Julia Taylor's vivid illustrations capture Jacob's day from one SPLAT! to another, culminating in him learning a valuable lesson about the importance of empathy. Teachers and adults are drawn to this interactive story.

Things That Go Where They Shouldn't

Rosie, a little girl liked by everyone, has a dream that results in some mischievous and unpredictable behaviour on her part. This rhyming story about the reaction of others when Rosie puts things in places they should not be is highly entertaining. There is also a lesson to be learned about consequences of one's actions.

Young readers happily imagine amusing scenarios of things they might put in places where they should not be. Not only children but teachers and parents are drawn to this interactive story.

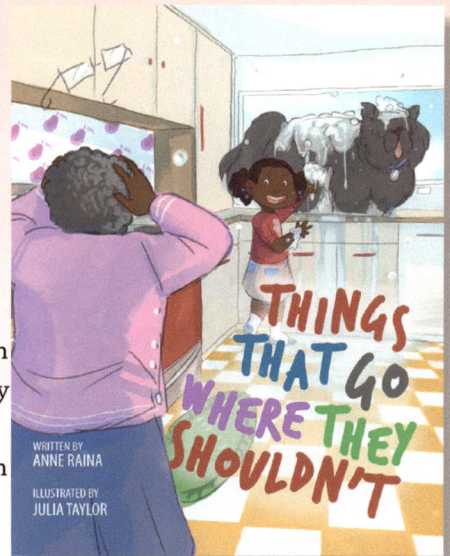

ISBN:
Paperback – 978-0-9867108-6-5
Hardcover – 978-0-9867108-5-8

BOOTH 15 # Rhoan Flowers

I have 7 books, Informer/The Wars Of Men, Informer 2/The Treachery Of Friends, Informer 3/Bloodshed Never Ends, Yahweh, Mama Devow, The Blue Jay And The Squirrel and The Volcano King.

Informer Trilogy

Is a biker novel that tells about the lives of two Caribbean men who re-located to Canada and eventually engaged in the biggest gang war in the country's history.

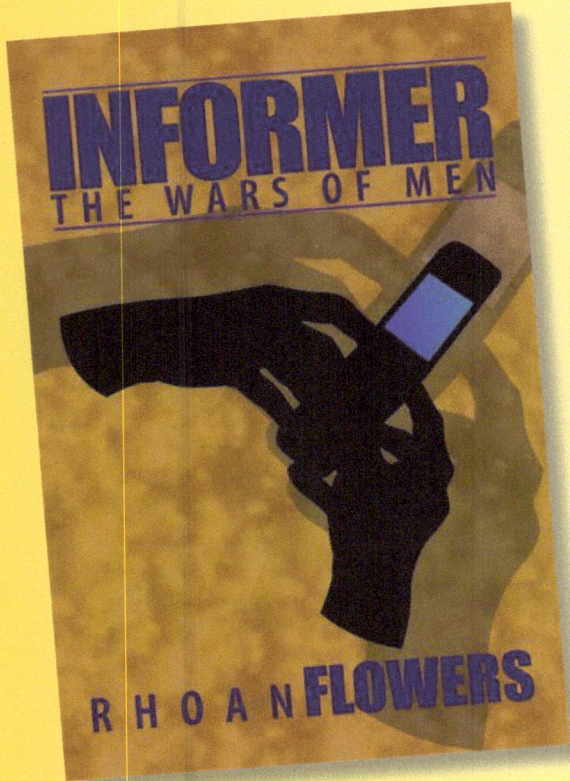

Informer/The Wars Of Men... ISBN 978-1-4490-4168-7

Informer 2/The Treachery Of Friends... ISBN 978-14969-4869-4

Informer 3/Bloodshed Never Ends... ISBN 978-0-2288-1097-1

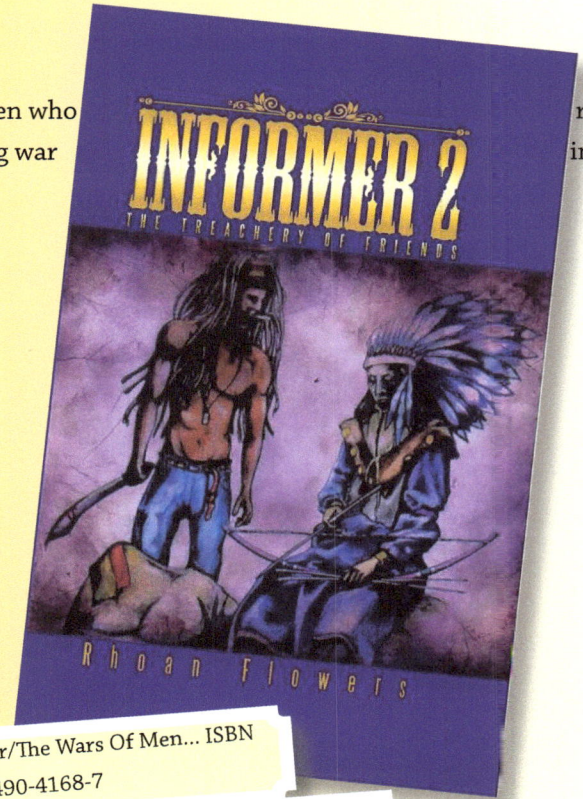

Yahweh

Is about God's return to reclaim the Earth, wherein angels from Heaven battle Satan's forces here on Earth.

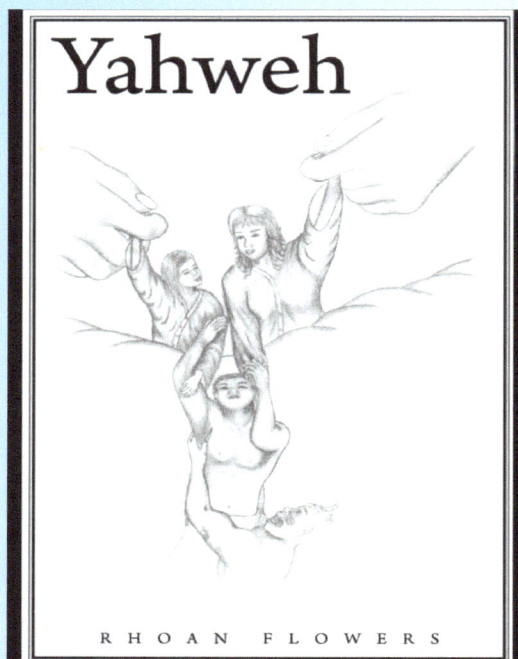

Mama Devow

Is about a Jamaican witch, whose time has come to surrender her powers to the family's heir, but refuses to surrender her powers because the child was taken abroad.

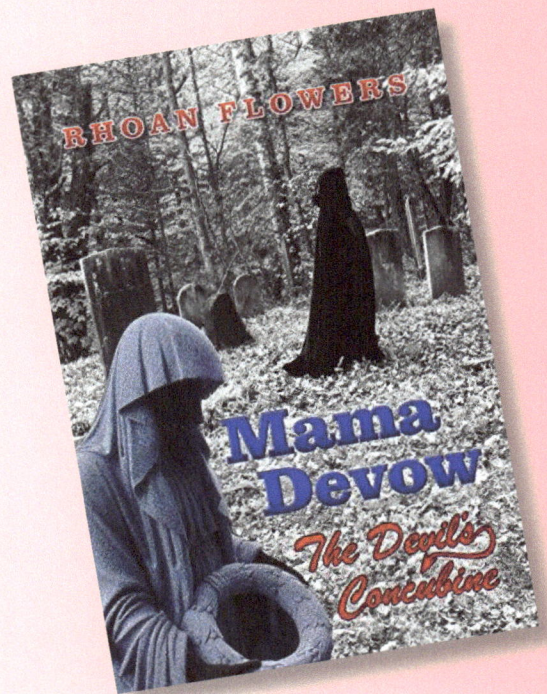

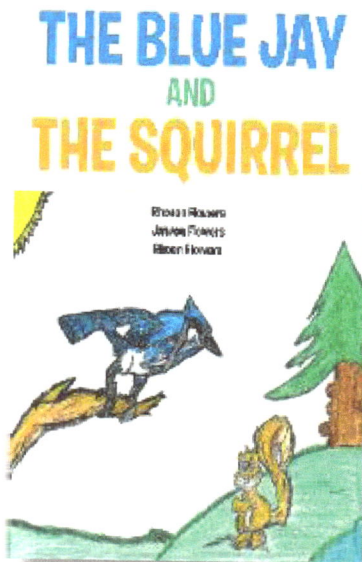

The Blue Jay And The Squirrel

Is a children's book about a bird who moved into a tree but the squirrel who lived there wants her to move immediately. All picture included in the book were drawn by my twin sons who were 9 years old at the time.

The Volcano King

Is my second children's book, and is about a group of captured animals that must save escape and save their homeland. Similar to the first, all the pictures included were drawn by my 11 year old sons.

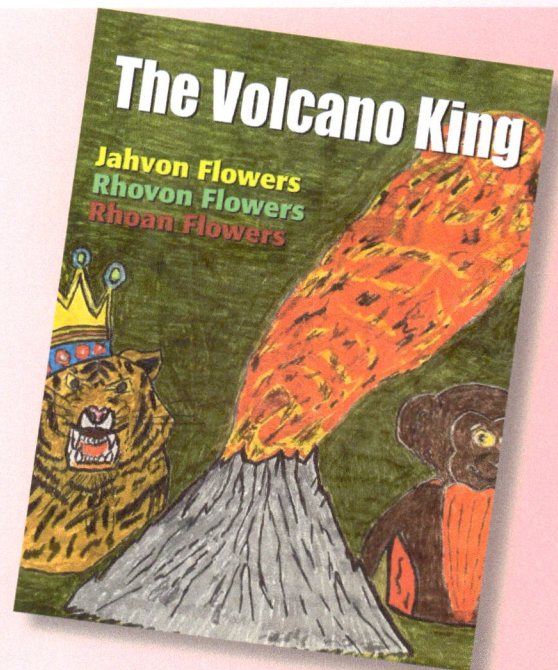

BOOTH 16

Hagit Hadaya

The author, Hagit Hadaya, has called Ottawa home since 1980. She holds a High Honours BA in Architecture/Art History and a Master's degree in Canadian Heritage Conservation, both from Carleton University, Ottawa.

Other books by author: *In Search of Sacred Space: Synagogue Architecture in Ottawa* (2013).*At Home With The Prime Minister: Ottawa Residences of the Prime Ministers Prior to 1952* is 135 pages, and includes more than 95 black-and-white historical photographs, endnotes, and bibliography.

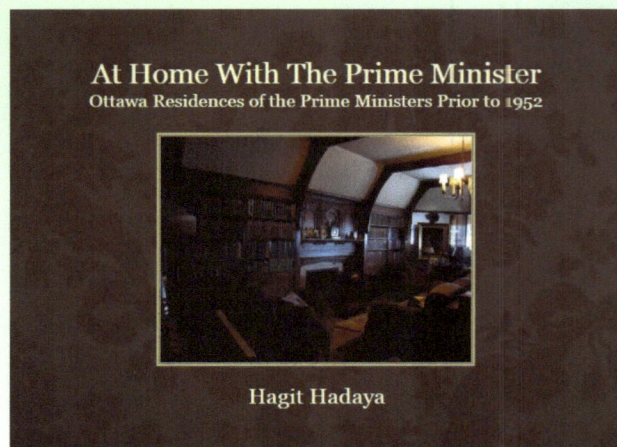

At Home With The Prime Minister
Ottawa Residences of the Prime Ministers Prior to 1952

Hagit Hadaya

E-mail address:
athomewithPM@gmail.com

BOOTH 18

Agora Books

Infinite Shades of Happiness:
Love & Online Dating
Revised Edition

By André Prince de Grâce

"Infinite Shades of Happiness: Love & Online Dating," by author André Prince de Grâce, is a new and fascinating book about what women are looking for in a relationship, and the communication barriers that still exist between men and women, especially on dating websites.

"Infinite Shades of Happiness" isn't a book about fake dating profiles, catfishing, or online predators but acknowledge its existence. This is a captivating page-turner, a study of real-life accounts from the men and women who went online, posted a profile, and braved the responses as they searched for (as author Prince de Grâce puts it) "the heart of their lives."

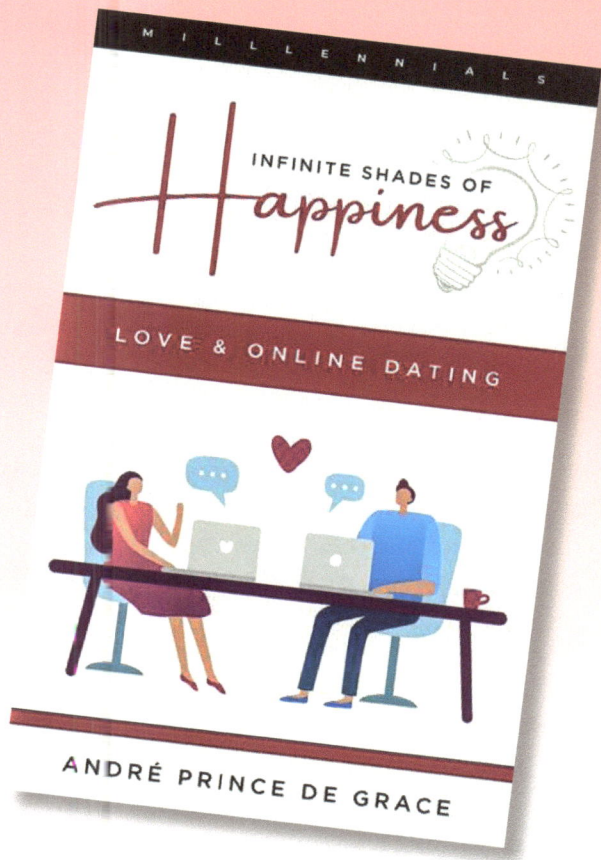

Little Cricky

by *Domnita Georgescu–Moldoveanu*
Translated and edited by Liliana Hoton

Little Cricky, a children's book by Domnita Georgescu-Moldoveanu, is a story in verse of a little cricket's adventures, translated from Romanian by Liliana Hoton and Miruna Nistor, whose children wereits first avid readers.

The author is a Romanian who emigrated to France during communism, and passed away in Paris in 2013. She began writingat an early age, and tried different genres: news, children's tales, novels, poems... She was a member of the Writers' Union from Romania, but it was in French that she wrote the majority of her work. After her death, her sister wished to continue publishing her posthumous work and convey the values that the author loved.

Each of us can live more or less happy

ISBN: 978-1-927538-33-3

What author André Prince de Grâce shows us is that with all of the infinite possibilities that online dating opens up, the old dating rituals are still firmly in our heads. Nevertheless, through his own online dating experiences and also through those of the many women he interviews, Prince de Grâce makes sense of it all and presents a universal look at the process of searching for a soulmate on dating websites.

The result is an amazing and unique book about the modern rules of online dating that is insightful, reassuring, and a must-read for anyone who is looking for a meaningful relationship on the internet.

ISBN: 978-1-927538-38-8

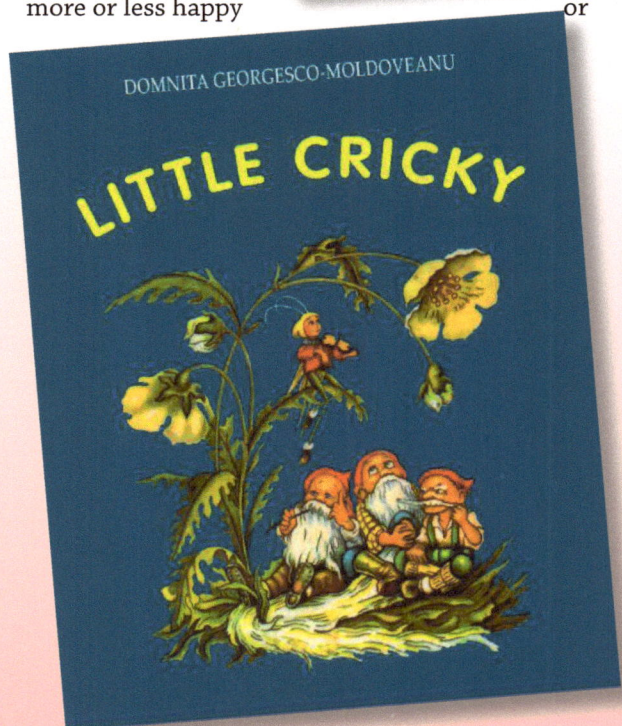

beautiful moments in our childhood, but all such moments certainly have an impact on us. Reading a book like Little Cricket is one of the marvellous moments a child can remember with fondness later in life. We all remember the strong feelings we experienced whenever we read a beautiful, meaningful book in our childhood. Little Cricket can take a child through a journey of feelings: joy, sadness, anger, anticipation, expectation, and most important, love of life!

Every page of the book speaks about not giving up, no matter the adversity: a good lesson for anyone, especially for a child. Not to mention the universal values that the story of the little cricket underlines: the beauty of the soul, loyalty, friendship, courage, passion, happiness.

The book is a little cricket's journey in search of his violin, which was stolen by the winter wind. We invite the little readers and their parents to embark upon this beautiful journey, illustrated in beautiful pictures. *Happy reading!*

NOT GONNA WRITE POEMS

A POETRY BOOK FOR ALL THE NON-POETS

Poems by Michael A. Lee
& Drawings by Michael and Jessica Lee

Not Gonna Write Poems:
A Poetry Book for All the Non Poets (paperback)

By Michael A. Lee

Michael A. Lee, a physician turned poet, has released his debut book of humorous children's poetry and sketches, titled Not Gonna Write Poems: A Poetry Book for All the Non Poets.

Dr. Lee's book is a collection of unique, witty poems and illustrations meant to be read out loud and enjoyed by both children and adults of all ages. This poetry book was inspired by his family' slove of the poems and drawings of Shel Silverstein, and it was co-illustrated by Dr. Lee's young daughter, Jessica.

Unlike some poetry books, Not Gonna Write Poems is not meant to be melancholy or serious; it introduces children to the world of poetry with funny verses and illustrations.

Children are inspired to read poetry, and perhaps to write it themselves, after they read Dr. Lee's poems about such subjects as homework to snoring to slime to "Whatever Happened to Superman?"

ISBN: 978-1-927538-44-9 (Paperback)
ISBN: 978-1-927538-45-6 (e-book)

Astroglossary
Revised Edition

By G Cyr

Mr Cyr had a great love for life, people and our planet. He touched the lives of everyone he

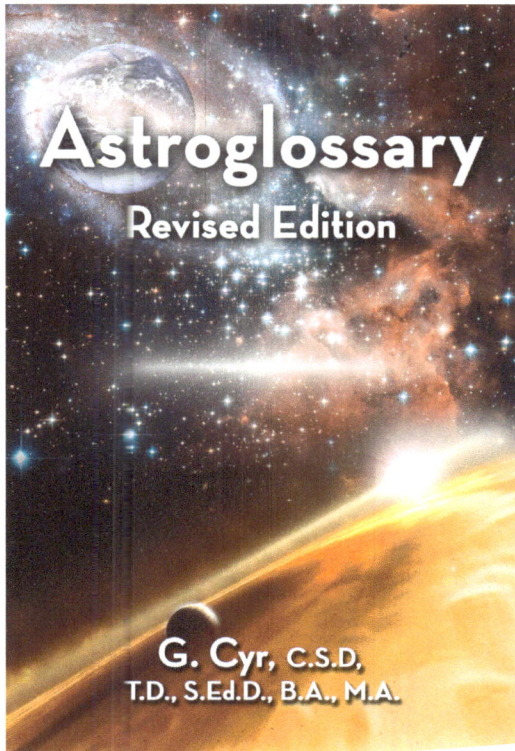

ISBN: 978-1-927538-34-0

met, and he had sought to inspire us, as humans, to re-connect with each other.

The world of science, and specifically, astronomy became one of Mr Cyr's biggest passions. It was Mr Cyr's vision in preparing this Astroglossary to inspire a new generation in our awakening as members of this great universe. Mr Cyr also shared a deep appreciation of the need to act as socially responsible custodians of our planet.

Knowing critical terms which help to educate us in the wonders of this universe is a first step in pursuing the kind of advanced knowledge of our universe and our place in it which will hopefully enable us all to share in a needed new direction in this cosmos.

However, it has been the perseverance of Ms Cyr, his wife, that we have to thank into re-kindling her husband's spirit which lives on in the revised edition of the Astroglossary.

Justin Trudeau, Judicial Corruption and the Supreme Court of Canada:
Aliens and Archons in Our Midst

By Peter Tremblay

Justin Trudeau, Judicial Corruption and the Supreme Court of Canada: Aliens and Archons in Our Midst takes us on a journey from the alleged corruption revealed by former Minister of Justice and Attorney General of Canada, Jody Wilson-Raybould to alien manipulation in

ISBN: 978-1-927538-41-8

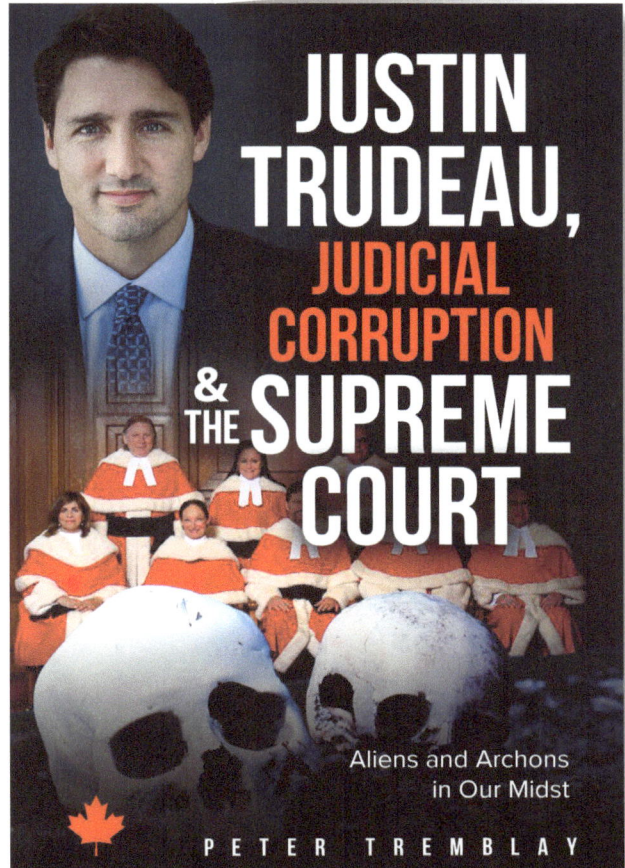

the guise of human faces. Such manipulation that has been reported by different reliable sources which include Dr. Michael Salla and the former Canadian Defence Minister Paul Hellyer. This manipulation context appears to include the apparent "Mandela Effect" AI orchestration.

In this book, Peter Tremblay uses judicial proceedings involving the Carby-Samuels case to substantiate the apparent existence of alien manipulation through strategically placed Archons.

It was John Lash who had documented in Metahistory.org ancient Pagan Gnostic insights of the Archons as an 'artificial intelligence' which is the product of cloning technology.

Have we as humans yet to come in contact with other sentient life forms in our universe as the elites would have us believe?

In mountains of evidence that this is simply not the case, veteran investigative journalist Peter Tremblay who has worked for former Canadian Defence Minister Paul Hellyer, brings together journalistic reports on a co-ordinated and apparent conspiracy among manipulative aliens and their Archon fronts. Such "Archons" appear to operate as "fifth columns" embedded within the police, the judiciary, and other institutions of governance in a similar way that terrorists can operate "sleeper cells" within various organizations.

Through judicial proceedings involving the Carby-Samuels case that have been documented by various investigative journalists who have worked with Peter Tremblay, the operation of aliens through their Archons are revealed. This book documents a path of alien manipulation and intrigue in relation to DezrinCarby-Samuels along with her husband Horace Carby-Samuels and the efforts of theirson to seek a pursue of his mother's liberation from apparent Archons.

MsCarby-Samuels has been subjected to apparent forcible confinement under an apparent regressive alien paralysis which has resulted in her not being able to walk, talk or write anymore.

Peter Tremblay has worked many years in government right up to Minister's Offices and also with all major Canadian political parties and has observed a pattern of manipulation which seems to subvert our human identity as beings of love, empathy and peace into a context of corruption through a system of justice that this book documents.

As this book reveals, the corruption which played out in the Canadian Justice system through the SNC-Lavalin Scandal between the Offices of the Prime Minister and Minister of Justice is only the tip of the iceberg or a sea of apparent corruption which undermines the desire of Canadians to pursue a society based upon social justice, ethics, due process and the rule of law.

In general, it is apparent that our world has little help to realize a desire of the values of our democracy and the environmental protection as long as these reported regressive aliens are allowed to infiltrate power structures in a manner which conflicts with our values as forward-thinking human beings.

Les Adolescents (cœur D'or)
– 2nd Edition

By Domnita Georgescu-Moldoveanu

Les Adolescents, c'est l'histoire de jeunes filles éduquées dans un pensionnat et qui font face à de mul-

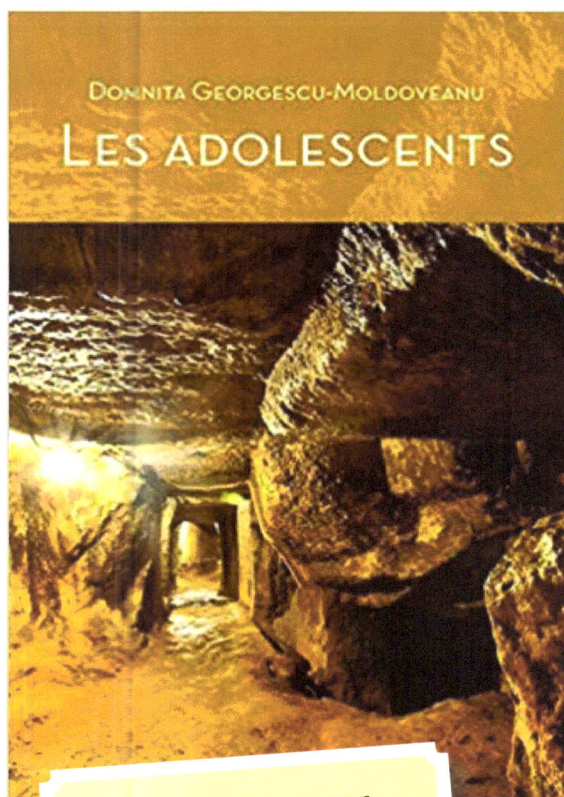

ISBN: 978-1-927538-03-6

minières en Roumanie, l'histoire de générations qui s'effritent, victimes du temps et de la malveillance.

La mère d'Anne est morte. Suicide ou assassinat? Et qui est son vrai père? Devenue orpheline, Anne est prise en charge par sa tante Marie, enseignante dans un pensionnat venant à peine de ré-ouvrir ses portes après l'occupation de 47. Anne découvre une famille unie et heureuse d'où elle s'enfuira brièvement, encore sous le choc de sa douleur. La famille Dona accueillera non seulement leur nièce Anne, mais aussi la mystérieuse Ilèana. Anne sera-t-elle rongée par la jalousie face à la popularité de sa nouvelle demi-sœur Auréline? Et qui est cette mystérieuse Ilèana à la voix d'or? Était-elle une princesse dans un passé encore si récent?

Le roman de Moldoveanu se lit comme un roman policier où devra se démêler la vérité parmi la cruauté des hommes. C'est un roman passionné, truffé de symboles et d'images poétiques, voire musicales, autant de reflets d'une Transylvanie d'après guerre au sein de paysages à la fois lumineux et lugubres.

tiples dilemmes moraux, des jeunes qui cherchent un sens à la vie. Mais c'est aussi l'histoire de ces villes

BOOTH 20 Danielle Wong

Poetry that Paints What Life Can Be Like with a Child Who Has Special Needs

There is a growing number of people with Autism. It is easy to come across people who know someone who lives with a person with Autism. Only those who live with it in their house day after day can understand what it truly means.

Parents are often treated like they are wrong to feel like the rug was pulled out from under them, they shouldn't feel isolated, they don't really need any extra support. They should be able to live exactly like all other parents. However, this is often how these parents feel: everything they expected is gone, they feel alone, they need people around them who can give them the extra help they need, and they need a society that understands.

Each person with Autism is unique. What they can learn on their own and what they cannot differs for each one. Many things that we take for granted that the child will learn eventually has to be taught. The child might have to be taught the meaning of every word, no matter how concrete, no matter how abstract, no matter how related it is to basic placement. The child might have to be taught how to watch other people's behaviour, to understand when to stop, when not to step over the line that will bring unwanted attention. The child might have to be taught there are more than just two emotions. This requires a lot of time and can leave the parent with little energy for anything else.

People with Autism are also frequently misunderstood. Most people see the reactions of people with Autism as exaggerated, as a sign of being spoiled,

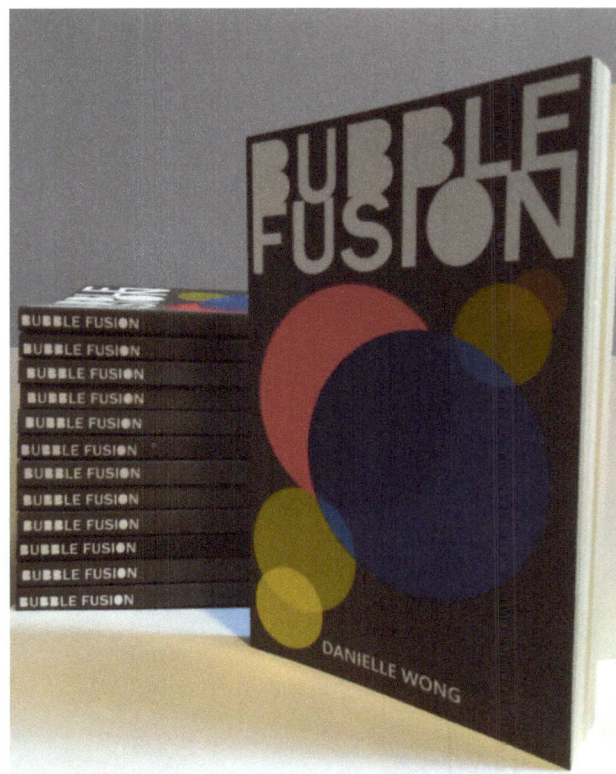

even as a plea for attention. However, people with Autism have the daunting task of having to figure out how they work best internally, what is expected of them in the external world, and how to build the

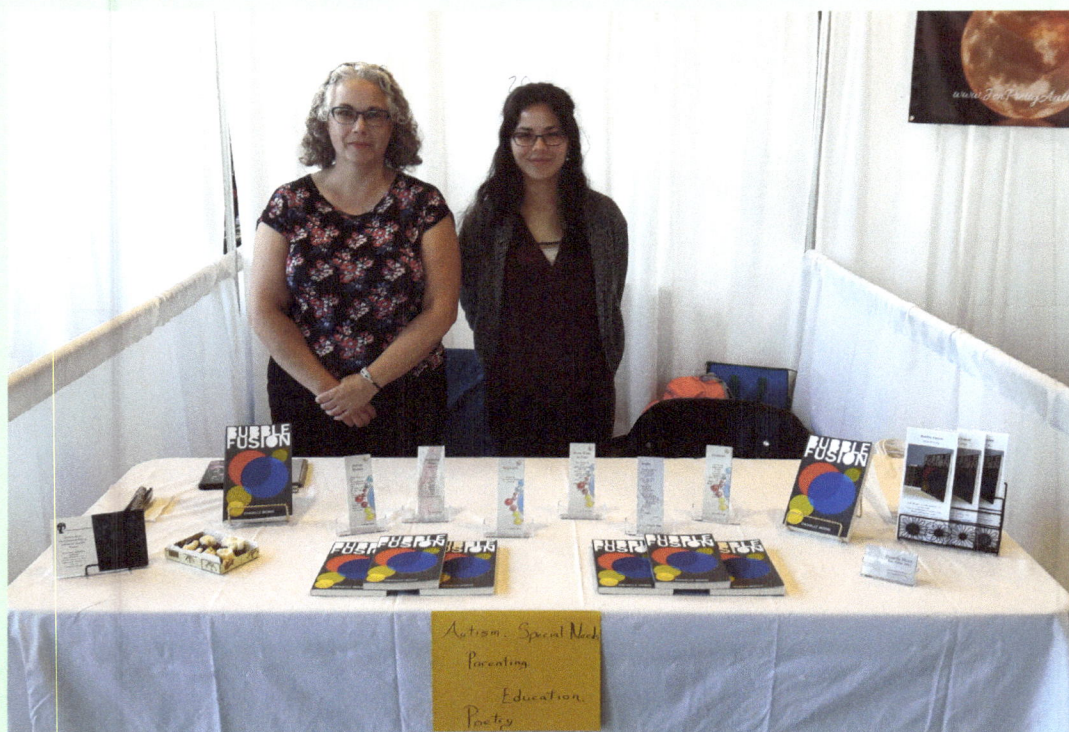

bridge between these two worlds. It can be overwhelming.

Bubble Fusion, by Danielle Wong, paints a portrait of a child with Autism from birth to early adulthood and her mother through a series of poems. It is set in three parts: "Inside One Bubble", "Inside an Un-suspecting Bubble", and "Time Ticks Inside Bubbles".

The first part, "Inside One Bubble", snapshots what it was like to have a newborn who didn't have the same reaction as her siblings at the same age, the acceptance of that child, and the attempts to keep up with the free quirkiness of the daughter. It shows how the child reacted to her world and her frustration as she came to realize she was not the same as the other children in class.

The second part, "Inside an Un-suspecting Bubble", focuses on the mother:what she endured, how her life changed, how she felt, how she spent her days.

The third part, "Time Ticks Inside Bubbles", is a coming to terms that finds all the good that happened. The original thoughts and dreams from the beginning were erased. They had to be. They were replaced with a more open outlook of life, an outlook that could only build stronger relationships and a surprisingly more beautiful life.

Bubble Fusion was written to look back over the years, come to terms with the situation, and to move on. Upon approaching the end of writing the book, it was clear that this book could help other parents just discovering this uncharted world, and it could help professionals working with children with special needs and their parents.

Danielle Wong has had her work published in various anthologies, Soft Cartel, Melinda Cochrane Publications blog, and Montreal Writes Literary Journal. She is a poet and author of flash to short fiction. She also is an editor, having worked on such books as *Unspoken* by Steven Fortune and *Pages in Time* by Gary Gurnsey. She currently lives in Montreal.

Bubble Fusion is available on Amazon and from Danielle Wong's website: https://daniellewong.ca.

I love this book of poetry!!! It's beautiful, moving, and powerful!! As a social worker I would recommend this book to anyone with a child with different needs and for anyone who works with families with children with different needs!! There are poems that really any parent can relate to!

– Wanda Nelson

Bubble Fusion by Danielle Wong is a beautiful collection of poetry that will allow you to more fully understand her daughter. She speaks honestly about being a special needs mom, and you can feel her joy, her complete love, and dedication in every single page. But she also talks openly about the struggles, especially in early diagnosis. Through her poetry, she allows everyone to see life through her daughter's eyes and her relationship to the world around her. Order a book, you won't be disappointed.

– Melinda Cochrane, President of Melinda Cochrane Publications Inc.

Jen Pretty

Jen Pretty is a local, prolific writer of smart urban fantasies. Her novels are character driven, witty, often violent, and with a liberal sprinkling of coarse language. Some of her books genre-hop into mythology, pulling characters and situations from a variety of sources.

She is going to read from her book Gargoyle Huntress, which released earlier this year and is now a complete trilogy. Gargoyle Huntress is a humorous paranormal novel with a bit of mystery and a whole lot of bitey stone demons.

Adam Thomlison

A Thief, a Spy, and the Corpse Who Rode Shotgun

By *Adam Thomlison*

A Canadian public servant gives sensitive information, and her sensitive heart, to the Danes. Meanwhile, across town, a small-time criminal with a loser's lust for winning is leveraging his nuts against the biggest score of his life.

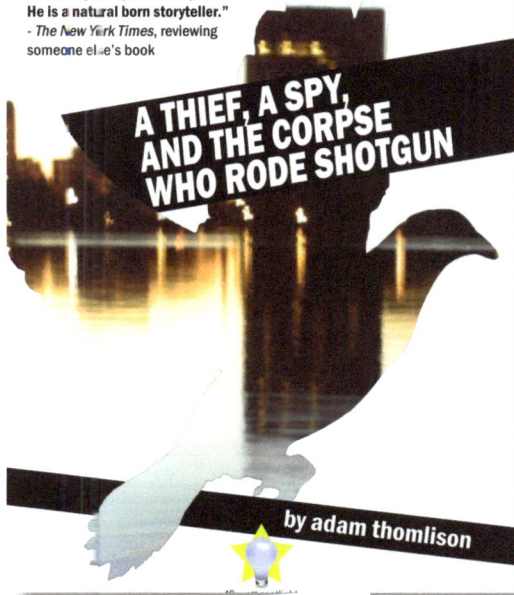

A THIEF, A SPY,
AND THE CORPSE
WHO RODE SHOTGUN

by adam thomlison

ISBN: 978-0-9738069-2-2

When their twisted and dishonest paths converge at the front door of a condo tower, will they – and their flexible, low-interest mortgage rates – survive?

Adam Thomlison's writing has been called "sparse and luminescent," and "a concentrated burst of humour and melancholy." He's the author of a book of short stories and an ongoing zine series, and the editor of an anthology of short screenplays.

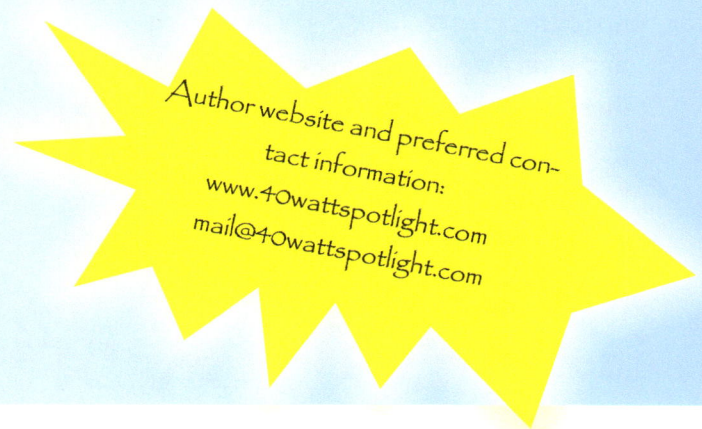

Author website and preferred contact information:
www.40wattspotlight.com
mail@40wattspotlight.com

BOOTH 23

Sally Tibbits and Meghan Tibbits

Badger Tales Wins Independent Publisher Award

Award winning author Meghan Tibbits and illustrator Sally Tibbits were thrilled to receive an Independent Publishers award for their first book Badger Tales: The Teacup Fliers! This past May, the mother-daughter team attended the awards ceremony at the iconic Copacabana Club in New York City.

Their first children's book is about two little mice who sail the skies in search of an adventure. But there's a catch: They aren't sure what an adventure is! Mr. and Mrs. Mouse soar their teacup parachute over dark forests, jagged mountains, and deep blue seas, seeking help from animals they meet along the way. In the end, they realize they were having an adventure all along!

Meghan explains, "Badger Tales" is inspired by the whimsical and imaginative artwork my mom painted when I was little. Growing up, my world was filled with fantastic creatures like the brave Mr. and Mrs. Mouse. "The Teacup Fliers" is based on two of her original paintings: Mrs. Badger reading from the book "Badger Tales", and two little mice flying a teacup parachute. Now that I am older, I am thrilled to bring her characters to life and put into words the stories I dreamed up for them as a child." " It's been a lot of work and a very steep learning curve", adds Sally, who illustrated this wonderful children's tale. "It's also been so much fun to be able to work on this project with my daughter."

Buoyed by the success of their first book, this dynamic duo have begun working on their second book in the series. We have a number of ideas that we are working on and we're looking forward to getting down to work on this next project.

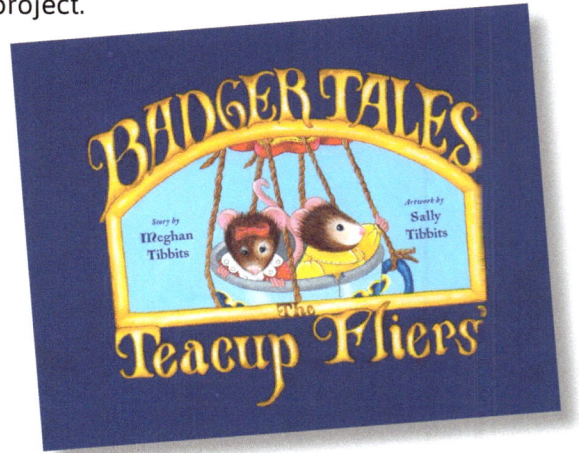

BOOTH 24 Jack Briglio

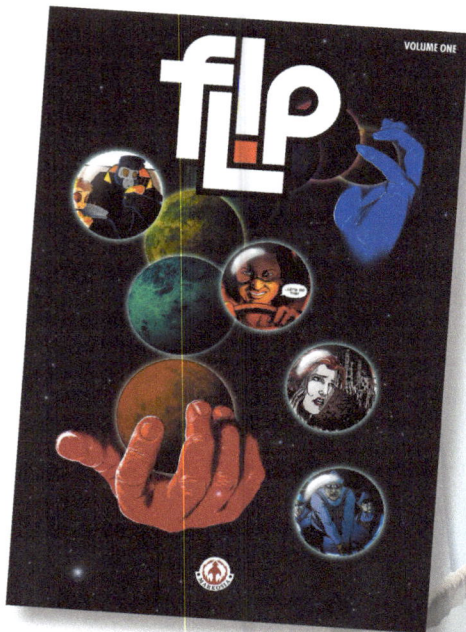

ISBN: 978-1-912700-33-2

Edited by Jack Briglio; Contributors - Jack Briglio and various writers and artists.

Flip is an anthology of alternate reality stories and flipped worlds, real-world what-ifs going against convention. Speculative fiction that examines our world and turns it on its head.

FLIP

Welcome to the monkey-eat-monkey flip world of luchador gorilla wrestling! Where fame is within reach... but a serious relationship seems miles and miles away.

Gorillas In The Ring – a magical relationship story by Derek Kunsken, Wendy Muldon & Ian Sharman.

<mark>FLIP</mark>

Welcome to a flip world where no one retires at an old age but instead enters the workforce much later than usual. Watch as this cop adventure brings new meaning to the words, young at heart!

Retire Early – by Marcello Bondi, Francesco Della Santa / Salvatore Coppola, & Alberto Massetti

<mark>FLIP</mark>

Welcome to a flip world psychological thriller where the smallest decision can have the biggest implications on the rest of your life...or death.

On Time – by Jack Briglio, Hugh Rookwood, Eleonora Dalla Rosa & Marvin S. Mariano.

<mark>FLIP</mark>

And finally, welcome to Flipworlds! Worlds slightly different from our own and worlds that Victor and Chiara control in their own way. What happens when they meet in a strange new Flipworld? Does love or hate rule the day?

Flipworlds – Unravel the mystery by Jack Briglio, Miguel Jorge, Eleonora Dalla Rosa & Ian Sharman.

Are all these stories flips of reality...or simply just stories about real life? Flip it over and find out...

Growing Up Enchanted
Vol 1: Fighting Bullies, Hunting Dragons

ISBN: 978-1-905692-38-5

By Jack Briglio & Alex Serra

FACT: Growing up is hard to do.

Fictional FACT: Growing up ENCHANTED is even harder to do!

The Eisner-nominated all-ages fantasy adventure series is back in print and finally collected as a trade! Join young Olianna and her family & friends as she tries to learn life's mundane lessons while practicing magic in a world of giants, trolls, and dragons!

Author website and preferred contact information:
Jackbriglio.com
jackbriglio@gmail.com

Bruce Foster

Bruce R. Foster is as semi-retired educator who continues to serve as an elementary principal on an intermittent basis. Indeed, he has been very fortunate to serve in a wide variety of roles during his upcoming sixth decade in education. He always finds his greatest joy is interacting with the students and their respective families. As such, Bruce has **incredible true experiences** to draw on from his encounters while primarily working as an administrator. He weaves a tale for his readers that honours the loveable nature of children and envelopes humanity, humour, and the fascinating yet highly unpredictable nature of being an educator.

Mr. Kool the title name of the main character in his four previous bilingual books, comes from one of those exact experiences when he encounters two grade three girls while assisting at yard duty. When asked if they remember his name, one curtly states, « Mr. Whatever! » The second girl politely says, « It is Mr. Kool with a « K » because you are always so kind to kids! »

This is the perfect title for the book's main character in Bruce's books, because as an educator, he believes that it is the natural, seamless relationship he builds with people and the way they touch his life that truly has a lasting impact.

Bruce and his wife Sandra live in Ottawa Ontario. They are proud parents of two adult children, and four very active grandchildren.

www.mrkool.ca is his remarkable website.

Bruce is delighted to announce that a portion of the sale of each book will continue to support Kids Help Phone (Canada), 1~800~668~6868. The M.S Society (Canada) 1~800~268~7582 will also receive a portion of the sale of each book.

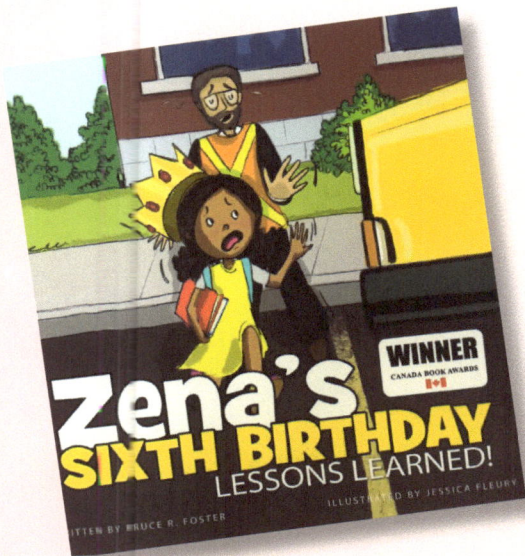

Zena's Sixth Birthday
Lessons Learned!

This unique TRUE storied children's picture book deals with a special sixth birthday for a grade 1 student. All of the day's pleasantries almost turn into a terrible tragedy, were it not for a very alert bus driver and helpful principal. Miniature Mr. Kool is a challenge for the reader to find as he is carefully hidden on each page containing a large illustration.

Zena's Sixth Birthday-Lessons Learned!
ISBN 978-0-9951758-2-2

Wild Times at Kool's School
Lessons Learned!

Wild Times At Kool's School-Lessons Learned ISBN 978-0-9951758-6-0

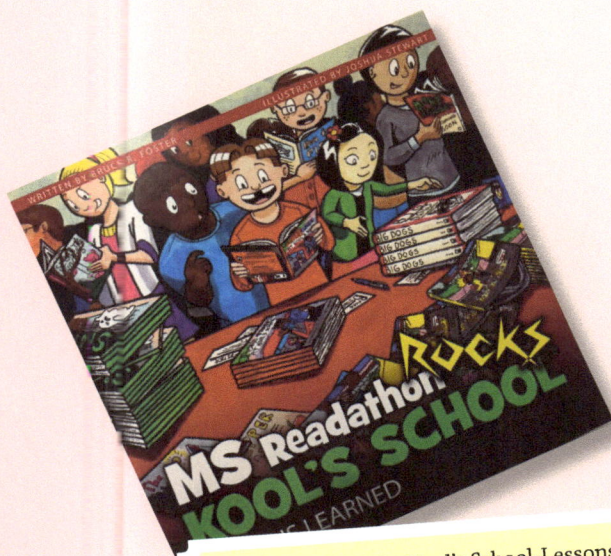

This exciting book focuses on a school-wide Crazy Hair Spirit Day. A concert by musician Yaki, really gets the students stimulated. Sadly, the good times are marred by a bullying incident that sees the principal respond quickly to the event. The book features 10 surefire ways for children to minimize bullying incidents.

MS Readathon Rocks Kool's School
Lessons Learned!

This classic highlights students' willingness and perseverance to both read and collect funds for an excellent charitable cause Their hard work is acknowledged as both the principal and vice-principal reward the pupils in a unique manner. The book provides children 10 tips to better understand Multiple Sclerosis as it affects adults.

Ms Readathon Rocks Kool's School-Lessons Learned ISBN 978-0-9951758-8-4

BOOTH 30   Anna Myatt

I am Jack

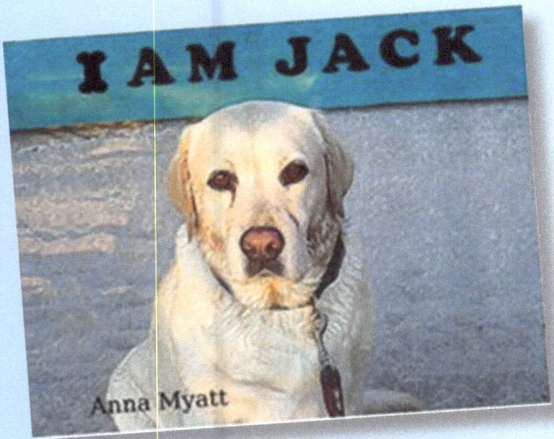

ISBN 978-1-77216-113-7

https://www.facebook.com/
greatbookforkids/

BOOTH 31   Armand Konan

L'univers Rêvé

It is a science fiction short story about a young man who enters into a parallel universe into which his thoughts materialize. In that reality he gets to face and overcome his biggest fears.

As the book is in French, here's the official Synopsis: "Eliam a peur d'assumer pleinement sa vocation d'artiste. Il se retrouve alors subitement plongé dans une réalité parallèle façonnée par ses pensées les plus intimes, qui prennent forme sous ses yeux. Pour survivre dans cet « Univers Rêvé », il devra vaincre un ennemi qui n'est autre que la personnification de ses peurs."

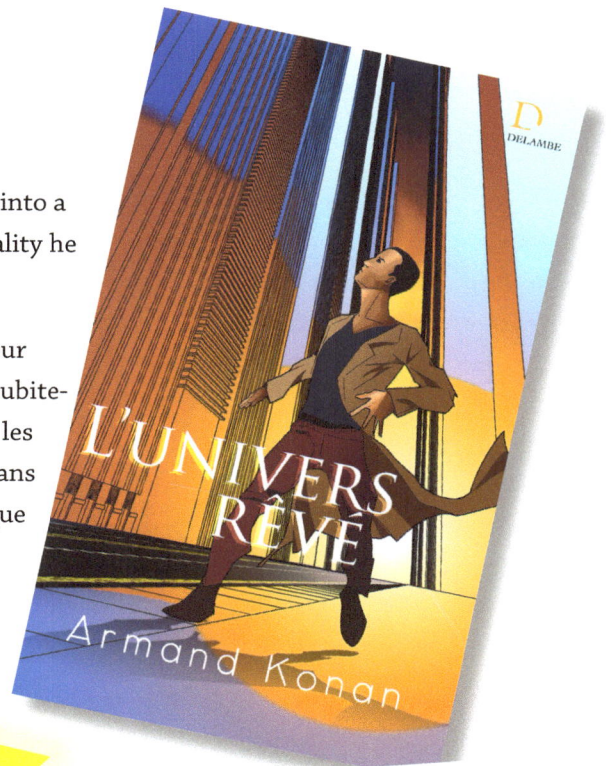

Author website and preferred contact information: www.luniversreve.com (This is the book website that has a section on the author)
For now www.armandkonan.net and www.armandkonan.com points to my book website but by your event these address will be up and running

ISBN
Paperback: 978-1-9990858-0-3
eBook: 978-1-9990858-1-0

BOOTH 33 — Robert Barsky

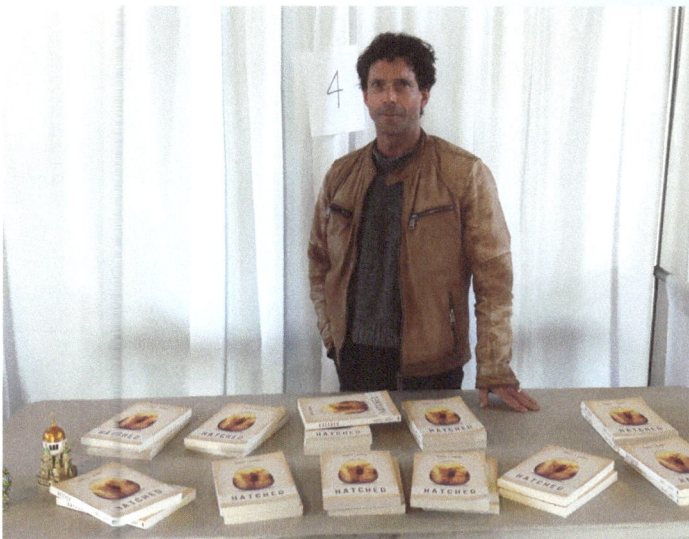

Robert Barsky paid some of his college bills by working in restaurants in Cape Cod and Montreal, and after graduating he moved to Switzerland to pursue a career in skiing, supporting himself by working in an upscale hotel bar. He now enjoys cooking for his wife and his college-aged children, and writing about language, literature and revolution. He is the author of eight books, including biographies of Noam Chomsky and Zellig Harris. This is his first novel, and he is excited (egg-cited?) to work on the next one.

Hatched

A well-respected chef in New York City has decided to fulfill a lifelong dream, to open a restaurant that is devoted entirely to "eggy" creations in the smart Wall Street area of the City. Working with an inspired architect, John erects his restaurant in the shape of a Fabergé egg, modeled after those remarkable masterpieces that were offered each year by the Czar to his beloved wife in the years leading up to the Russian Revolution. Fabergé Restaurant becomes 'the' destination for the wealthiest of NYC clients, but it's also the place where a plan is Hatched by three former college roommates to counterfeit billions of dollars and shake the United States economy to its very yolk. A rollicking novel filled with intrigue, passion and voluptuous egg recipes, Hatched is a sumptuous treat.

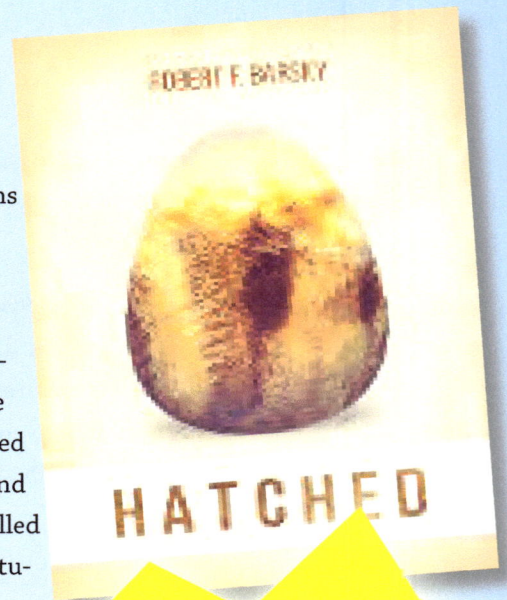

Professor Robert Barsky,
Canada Research Chair: Law, Narrative and Border Crossing
Department of Law and Legal Studies
Room C473 Loeb Building
Carleton University
Ottawa, ON K1S 5B6 Canada

BOOTH 34 Peacock Press

When the Poet Met the Publisher to Co-create Peacock Press and 'Because I Can'

Once upon a time, two people – who had only recently met each other but had known all along that they would become friends for life – were having a heartfelt conversation.

One was an aspiring publisher and the other a budding poet.

The poet had never shown her work to anyone because it was so personal and heart-rending. The publisher-to-be had been sharing her hopes and dreams with everyone she met, even when they laughed in her face as soon as she revealed her "ambitious plan" to start a publishing company some day.

The conversation between the poet and publisher that day led to many things (more on that later!), including the realization that they could turn their supportive friendship into a constructive business relationship.

And this is how, ladies and gentlemen, Peacock Press was incorporated!

What followed (and are still on!) were many brain-storming sessions and sleepless nights

Hanieh Khoshkhou and
Shabana Ansari

working over content, design and strategy to not only publish a book of poetry but also run a successful publishing business.

The dynamic duo – Hanieh Khoshkhou and Shabana Ansari – are determined to make a difference, no matter how small, in the lives of everyone who shares their passion for well-written and well-designed books.

The co-founders of Peacock Press are passionate about telling stories that often go unheard and are committed to providing a platform to anyone who has ever felt marginalized or underrepresented. Through the books they publish and the stories they tell, Hanieh and Shabana are hoping to fill the diversity gap in publishing while starting meaningful conversations around the need for more inclusive storytelling.

They have recently released their first book "Because I Can", written by Hanieh, a collection of poetry and prose about love, longing, and living a full life despite all the odds. It is written as one-liners to read quickly, or at leisure depending on your mood, when you feel like you need to hear a voice not unlike your own.

Hanieh and Shabana look forward to meeting you at the Ottawa Book Expo on Sunday October 20 and talking at length about their publishing journey so far while proudly showcasing "Because I Can", the first of many more books that they hope to publish through Peacock Press.

"Because I Can" is also available on Amazon

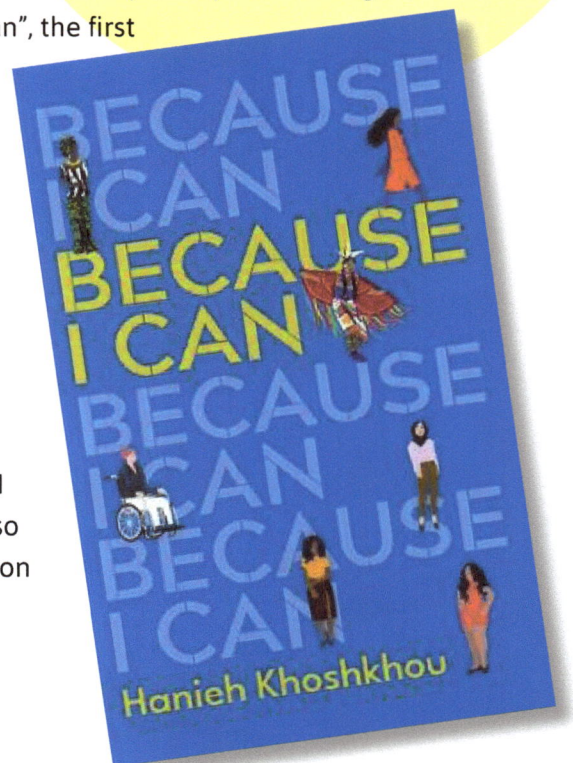

Ottawa Independent Writers (OIW)

Ottawa Independent Writers (OIW) was created in 1986 as a gathering place for people with a passion to weave fiction and non-fiction stories, write poetry and plays and string words together in a variety of other formats. OIW provides a venue where writers can share experiences and learn new aspects of their craft. We empathize with writers having trouble getting started and we celebrate with those whose works are published. Along the way, we give them the tools necessary to improve their work. Although the emphasis is on writing, we also focus on the business of writing, which includes finding a publisher, editing, cover design, promotion and marketing, networking and keeping track of finances. Writers who need help in any of these areas will be connected with members who can offer advice, or we can link them with outside experts. OIW serves the interests of all writers, from novice to seasoned scribe. Our members are involved in advertising, biography, business communications, children's literature, literary publicity, memoirs, translation, freelance writing, consumer affairs, drama, education, fiction and non-fiction, government, health, high technology, humour, magazines, music, mystery, journalism, novels, poetry, science, short stories, speculative fiction, speeches, screenwriting, travel and more!

Meghan Negrijn

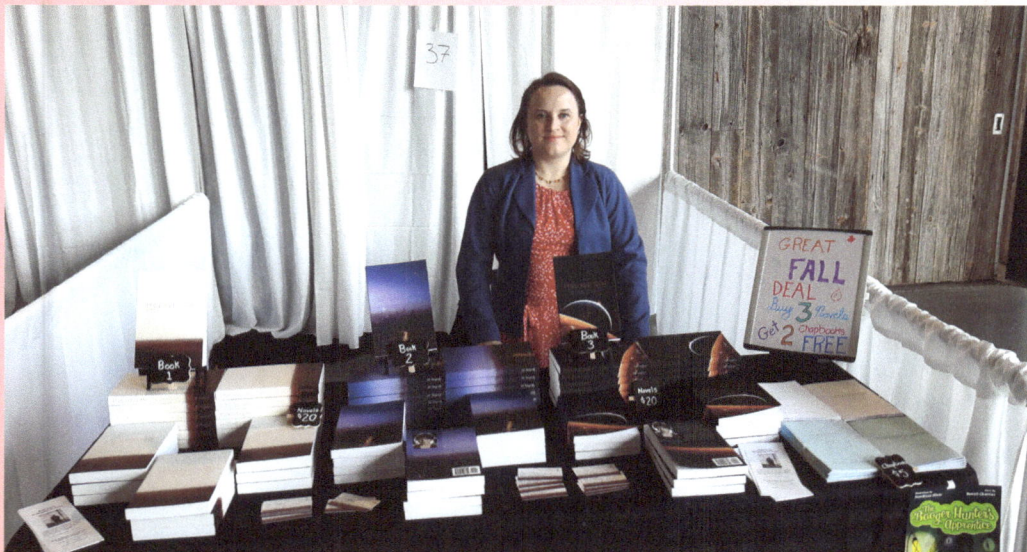

BOOTH 39

Obsidian Eagle

Inspired Canadian Anti-Poet Spins An Unconventional Epic Tale In His Latest Book

The people of Earth are being watched. But even more to the point, they are being physiologically altered without their knowledge. Not by extra-terrestrials, but by cosmic beings who have been exiled to the Earth's solar system by their most high oracular to live out their remaining days in solitary confinement.

This is the intriguing premise for the latest work of anti-poet turned meta-author Obsidian Eagle. In his newest book, titled *A Codex For Gnostics: A Cosmic Comedy*, writer Obsidian Eagle explores the possibilities of how cosmic and celestial forces, along with their belief systems and intergalactic struggles for power influence the lives of people on Earth – many times with earthlings none the wiser.

The story begins with Brax, the leader of six other rebel cosmic beings who, like the other six, has been convicted of attempting to overthrow the ruling leader of their home zone in the Megalocosmos. Consequently, the seven rebels are condemned to serve a life sentence in solitary confinement– each one on a separate orb in an isolated, backwater solar system - a solar system in which the planet Earth just so happens to also orbit. Brax is assigned to the sphere of Marz, while the other six rebels are dispersed to their own neighbouring orbs in the same solar system.

Not one to be stationary, Brax quickly finds a way to communicate with the others on their respective isolated orbs. During the course of their dialogues, Brax

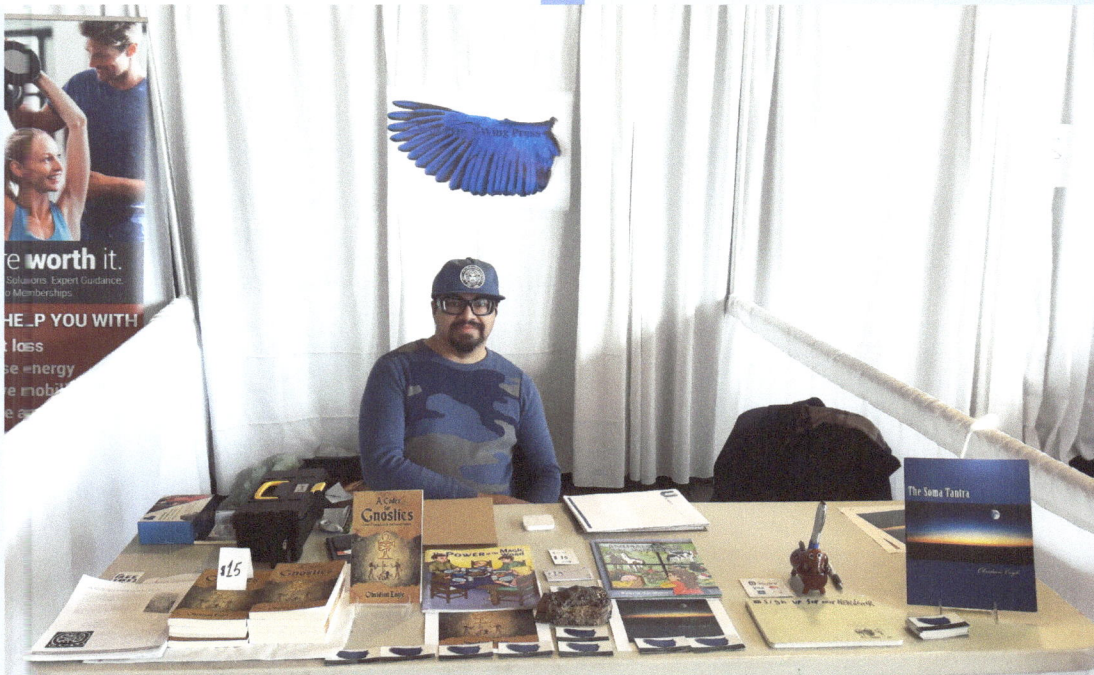

A Codex for Gnostics

Cosmic Comedy Writ In The Zone of Malkuth

Obsidian Eagle

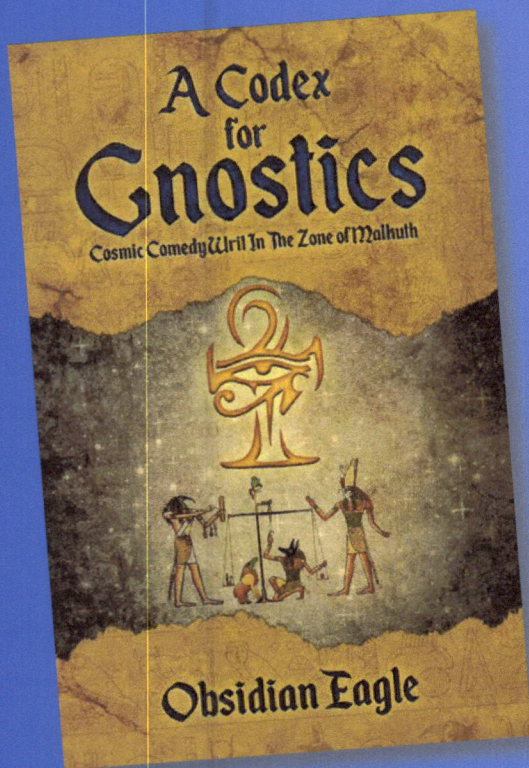

discovers the orb of Tellz (Earth), and it piques his interest. Here is a sphere in the dawn of existence - one that is full of primates whom he can physiologically alter and rule over - not seeming to remember that trying to direct the evolution of life in his own Megalocosmos is what got him exiled to Marz in the first place.

A Codex For Gnostics, the second installment in meta-author Obsidian Eagle's *Lunacy Trilogy*, is his most recent and also most untraditional offering to date. An epic story which combines the teachings of Kabbalah, Thelema, and Zoroastrianism, along with the study of Egyptology and other disciplines, *A Codex For Gnostics* is unlike any other epic narrative before it. Weaving together epic poetry with esoteric mysticism, meta-poet turned meta-author Obsidian Eagle creates an experimental work of fiction that is both metaphysical comedy and epic action, written on a cosmic level.

In the prologue, Obsidian Eagle paints quite a different picture of the universe as we know it. While Earth (Tellz) is in its infancy, one celestial being - Baal Abraxah (Brax for short) is out to rule the galaxies in his home zone of Ketheroz.

Brax already hails from a prominent line of Arkhonz (those who serve the Everlasting Presence dwelling at the heart of each galaxy in the zone of Ketheroz). However, even when he is young, Brax's own star shines brightly enough to rival that of the galactic core, which gives him a loaded God complex that is as large as the entire zone of Ketheroz. Brax foolishly thinks he is far superior to the oracular Amoun-Rah, the one who presides over Ketheroz by way of having manifested the highest form of Ayn Zoph Aur.

In order to start taking over, Brax recruits six others of Arkhonzian descent to establish their own version of Ayn Zoph Aur. They name it Heptap-arah-Parzhynokh, or the Law of Seven. After raising several large armies, the goal of deposing Amoun-Rah off the throne of Ketheroz so that Brax can rule in his place becomes crystal clear. However, the army is defeated near the galaxy centre before this can happen. Brax is personally defeated in an ultimate battle between himself and the powerful Archangel Azhah Vahyzthah.

It is then that Brax realizes the full authority of Amoun-Rah, and just how far the Will of Ayn Zoph Aur reaches throughout and even beyond their single universe. This is when he and the other insurgents are exiled to the backwater solar system they call Orz, where the planet Earth orbits, and where the real story begins. And little does anyone on Earth, including Dex, an ordinary daydreamer stuck in a dead-end job, realize they will eventually be dragged into a battle of intergalactic proportions between Archangels who pick up where Brax leaves off after he perishes.

It is Obsidian Eagle's writing style that makes the narrative of *A Codex For Gnostics* in no way typical of any current offerings in the science fiction or fantasy genres. If it is to be classified at all, the writings of Dante Alighieri would be a good place to start.

This is because Obsidian Eagle embraces so many of the religious and philosophical ideologies of alternative cultures; so he presents us with a mythical scenario that is further enhanced with beliefs garnered from many different schools of thought.

And while the theme of the book seems heavily philosophical, there is also quite a bit of humour in *A Codex For Gnostics* - and the comedy is what further separates this book from the rest of the pack. Starting with the subtitle "Cosmic Comedy Writ In The Zone of Malkuth," Obsidian Eagle continues to entertain his readers with a sharp wit and a sense of humour that makes this book a thoroughly enjoyable read. In addition, the book delivers relentless wordplay and isjam-packed with hidden references to bemuse even the savviest of readers.

But in order to fully appreciate *A Codex For Gnostics*, the revolutionary writing style of Obsidian Eagle needs to be explored a bit further. Looking at his first book in the *Lunacy Trilogy* gives more insight into the revolutionary writing style of Obsidian Eagle.

This first book in the *Lunacy Trilogy* entitled *The Soma Tantra: A CosmicTragedy* is about an age-old conflict between demonic Ashuras and godly Devatas, which is rekindled when the moon god Soma Chandra defies his brethren by kidnapping their Guru's new wife. And although the two stories are unrelated, the voice of Obsidian Eagle is unmistakable, and the struggle for the balance of power between mortals and immortals is the subject matter the two books share.

The third book in the trilogy, *Tome of The Sixth Sun: A Cosmic Dramedy*, is currently in the works.

BOOTH 40 Free Form Fitness

Free Form Fitness brings something new to the personal training studio niche of the fitness industry.

Free Form Fitness was started in Kanata and actually began as a large, big-box style gym. Although they focused on creating a supportive community, one that would encourage people at all ages and stages of their fitness journey to come and really enjoy working out, they found that the majority of people would use their memberships for a short period of time, and then slowly but surely decrease the consistency

of their workouts, until they were at a point where they never came in.

This is a story that is all too common of big box style, membership-based gyms. Without the accountability, members can easily "fall off the wagon", leaving their health and fitness to take a back seat to everything else that takes up their time.

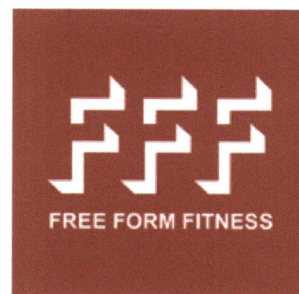

FREE FORM FITNESS

Instead of simply cashing the cheques and accepting the low-commitment rate they had, Free Form Fitness made the decision to turn their focus towards personal training.

It was in this decision that Free Form Fitness saw their first 1000 lives changed.

This incredible success, and the community that established itself within those early locations, gave FFF insight into what really worked and what didn't work with personal training. We observed, and listened, and adapted our training philosophy to match what we saw worked best.

After all the goal is to help individuals *realize their full health potential.*

One of the many barriers to people achieving their fitness goals is time. Ottawa is a busy city with busy professionals who not only have a professional life to manage, but a personal one as well.

This is why Free Form Fitness took the classic model of 45 minutes - 1 hour personal training sessions, and brought it down to 30 minutes. Now our clients could fit in a workout on their lunch break, before or after work, and in between errands like picking up and dropping off the kids at their activities.

Research has also shown time and time again that it only takes 30 minutes of focused, intentional, moderate intensity exercise to get the health benefits that exercise offers.

This is where our incredible trainers come in. We take great care in selecting the best-of-the-best trainers. Before being hired they are put through the paces with a 10-step interview process, complete with a test and mock session, where we actually evaluate their theoretical and practical knowledge.

Once hired, the trainers at Free Form Fitness create unique programs for every client. **There are no cookie-cutter, cut-and-paste programs at Free Form Fitness**. If every client is coming in with different exercise history, injuries, daily routines, and lifestyles, then our trainers need to provide a program that will suit those specifications.

This is why you see "Personal Trainers Who Care" on our logo. Our personal trainers listen first. **Our free consultation gives our trainers 30 minutes to sit down and just listen**. Once we have listened, we then process the information, match them up with the trainers that best fit their needs, and that client is given 8 sessions to decide if personal training is right for them. Those 8 sessions come at one of the lowest prices in the city - $96 (yes - that is the total price).

Although we do believe that personal training is the best way for anyone to learn about their body, their diet, and make improvements to their health and fitness that will last a lifetime, we also make sure that Free Form Fitness feels like the place to achieve their goals.

The fact is that the gym is a place where humans have to face the reality that they are weak, or that they may be in a place where they believe that who they are in the present is not good enough.

This is the final point that truly sets Free Form Fitness apart from all other personal training options. Although we establish areas that need improvement with our clients, every time a client steps into one of our 5 locations they know that everyone there believes they have the potential to be great. Free Form Fitness believes that everyone is enough, and they do have the potential to reach their greatest goals and live a truly healthy, and long life.

Every time a client arrives at Free Form Fitness is another opportunity not to be faced with the question of their self-worth, but to be faced with the reality that they've had it in them all along.

"Realize your full health potential" is our core message because it's what we believe at our core. *Potential energy* in physics is the energy that is stored within an object. A client's best self is already within them before they come to Free Form Fitness.

Through intelligent programming, caring trainers, and an incredibly supportive community, we facilitate the realization that their healthiest and strongest self has been within them their whole life.

Book Self-Publishing

Ottawa Book Self-Publishing Service Gives Writers New Local Alternative

Agora Publishing is one of the book self-publishing service providers that is giving new local writers in Ottawa an alternative to publishing their work. The presence of modern book self-publishing options has increased the arrays of options available to new writers.

One of the hardest challenges faced by new writers is usually trying to impress traditional publishers. With the new options available from **Agora Publishing** and similar self-publishing services, writers will not have to work so hard anymore. With the help of web-based publishing platforms and customized printing services, budding writers can chase publication and promotion of their book on their own.

Book self-publishing services allow the writer to retain the full intellectual property of their book.

One of the benefits of choosing **Agora Publishing** is that their publishing service is accessible to writers Canadian and international writers. They also have a lot of options to choose from so that you will not at any point feel as if an option is shoved down your throat. Inasmuch as self-publishing has its own challenges, there are lots of benefits that rules out the negatives. These include;

1. You are in Charge Creatively

Getting the nod of traditional publishers is big a challenge. Most times your manuscript never make it beyond the editor's table. When you finally get the acceptance letter, the editors may insist that you take out some of your favourite lines or rewrite the manuscript. When you are self-publishing or using self-publishing services, you decide what stays and what leaves. You can decide to employ the services of a professional at any stage (writing, editing, cover design, and printing) to meet your desired taste and standard.

2. You Keep a Larger Chunk of the Money

Your self-publishing platform may take a small percentage of your earning. However, this nominal is nothing compared to the arrangement in traditional publication. In the latter, the traditional publishers take a larger chunk of the money and pay you royalties. Since you get to keep a larger chunk of the money in self-publishing, you WWwill be able to pay for adverts to promote your book. Having a large social cycle also makes it easy for you to promote your work.

3. The Price is Under Your Control

When you are new to the field of writing, reading your work will almost be like a gamble for readers – because they are unsure if it is worth the investment. The higher the price of your book, the less likely the readers will be willing to gamble. If you set the price of your masterpiece too

low, it may also be misjudged by readers. You have to find the balance that will increase your readership as well as give some credibility to your work. The ostentatious price of some books from traditional publishers is the sole reason they never made it to the best-seller status.

4. Strengthen Your Reputation

Traditional publishers are becoming more averse to risk. They are becoming less willing to publish writers without some reputation in the field. The reason is simple; works from unpopular authors are more difficult to market. When you have a few self-published books that have made good sales, your chances of being accepted by a traditional publisher grows.

The journey towards self-publishing exposes the writer to lots of people which expands their network and guarantees that the writer can have their book in the open whenever they deem fit irrespective of the opinion of the traditional publisher. The journey to self-publishing can be a little stormy but you can calm the waves when you subscribe to **Agora Publishing**'s self-publishing services in Ottawa.